Intermediate Paper 9
Management Accounting – Decision Making

First edition 2002
Third edition January 2004

ISBN 0 7517 1490 9 (previous edition 0 7517 0267 6)

British Library Cataloguing-in-Publication Data

A catalogue record for this book is available from the British Library

Published by
BPP Professional Education, Aldine House, Aldine Place, London W12 8AW
www.bpp.com

Printed in Great Britain by Ashford Colour Press

All our rights reserved. No part of this publication may be reproduced, stored in a retrieval system or transmitted, in any form or by any means, electronic, mechanical, photocopying, recording or otherwise, without the prior written permission of BPP Professional Education.

BPP Professional Education
2004

Welcome to BPP's CIMA **Passcards** for Paper 9 *Management Accounting – Decision Making*.

- They **save you time**. Important topics are summarised for you.
- They incorporate **diagrams** to kick start your memory.
- They follow the overall **structure** of the BPP Study Texts, but BPP's CIMA **Passcards** are not just a condensed book. Each card has been separately designed for clear presentation. Topics are self contained and can be grasped visually.
- CIMA **Passcards** are **just the right size** for pockets, briefcases and bags.
- CIMA **Passcards focus on the exam** you will be facing.

Run through the complete set of **Passcards** as often as you can during your final revision period. The day before the exam, try to go through the **Passcards** again! You will then be well on your way to passing your exams.

Good luck!

		Page			Page
1	Information for decision making I	1	11	Further aspects of investment appraisal	131
2	Information for decision making II	7	12	Investment centre performance appraisal	147
3	Quantitative techniques	17			
4	Linear programming (simplex)	33			
5	Pricing	41			
6	Transfer pricing	59			
7	Relating costs to cost objects	67			
8	Standard costing	79			
9	Costing systems for modern manufacturing	97			
10	Investment appraisal: basic principles	113			

1: Information for decision making I

Topic List

Relevant costs

Assumptions and qualitative factors

It is important to realise that decision-making questions are likely to ask you to discuss 'other factors that should be considered' as well as require you to carry out calculations to support a particular decision option. So don't neglect these qualitative issues. And, as always, remember to state any assumptions you make.

> Key questions to try in the kit: 1, 3
> Refer to MCQ cards (with Ch 2): 1 - 20

	Relevant costs	Assumptions and qualitative factors

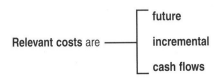

Relevant costs are — future, incremental, cash flows

Examples

Avoidable costs are costs which would not be incurred if the activity to which they relate did not exist.

A **differential cost** is the difference in total costs between alternatives.

An **opportunity cost** is the benefit which would have been earned, but which has been given up, by choosing one option instead of another.

The relevance of fixed costs

Unless given an indication to the contrary, assume fixed costs are irrelevant and variable costs are relevant.

- **Directly attributable fixed costs**, although fixed within a relevant range or regarded as fixed because management has set a budgeted expenditure level, are relevant because they do one of two things.
  - Increase if certain activities are undertaken
  - Decrease/are eliminated if a decision is taken to reduce the scale of operations/shutdown entirely
- **General fixed overheads** (such as an apportioned share of head office charges) are unaffected by a change in the scale of operations and are irrelevant.

Non-relevant costs

Cost	Description	Example
Sunk costs	Expenditure which has already been incurred and charged, or which has already been incurred or which which relates to an expenditure decision which has irrevocably been taken, and which will be charged in a future accounting period	Development costs already incurred
Committed costs	Future cash outflows that will be incurred regardless of the decision taken	Contracts already entered into
Notional costs	Hypothetical accounting costs which reflect the use of a benefit for which no actual cash expense is incurred	Notional rent
Historical costs		

Relevant costs | Assumptions and qualitative factors

Identifying relevant costs

Example

Machinery user costs
- Once a machine has been bought its cost is a sunk cost.
- Depreciation is not a relevant cost because it is not a cash flow.
- Using machinery may involve some relevant incremental user costs (hire charges, fall in resale value of owned assets).

Example

Materials
- The relevant cost is generally current replacement cost.
- If materials have been purchased but will not be replaced, the relevant cost is the higher of the following.
  - Current resale value
  - Value if put to an alternative use
- If there is no resale value and no other use, the relevant cost is nil.

Example

Labour
- Costs are often not incremental because the labour force will be paid irrespective of the decision made.
- If the labour force can be put to an alternative use, the relevant cost is the sum of the following.
  - The variable costs of the labour and associated variable overheads
  - The contribution forgone from not being able to put the workforce to its alternative use

Relevant cost of a scarce resource = contribution / incremental profit forgone from the next best opportunity for using the scarce resource (**opportunity cost**) + variable cost of the scarce resource (cash expenditure to purchase it, if it has not already been purchased)

Example

Relevant cost per hour of scarce machine time = contribution per hour from hiring out a machine as opposed to using it + running cost per hour of the machine

Relevant costs and minimum pricing

The minimum price for a one-off product or service contract is its total relevant cost. This is the price at which the company would make no incremental profit and no incremental loss from undertaking the work, but would just achieve an incremental cost breakeven point.

| Relevant costs | **Assumptions and qualitative factors** |

Assumptions in relevant costing

- Cost behaviour patterns are known.
- The amount of fixed costs, unit variable costs, sales price and sales demand are known with certainty.
- The objective of decision making in the short term is to maximise 'satisfaction', which is often regarded as 'short-term profit'.
- The information on which a decision is based is complete and reliable.

Qualitative factors in decision making

- The availability of cash
- Employees
- Customers
- Competitors
- Timing factors
- Suppliers
- Feasibility
- Flexibility and internal control
- Unquantified opportunity costs
- Political pressures
- Legal constraints
- Inflation

2: Information for decision making II

Topic List

- Joint cost allocations
- Make or buy decisions
- Either/or problems
- Shutdown decisions
- Operational gearing

Decision-making questions will build on the knowledge you gained in your earlier studies and, as well as requiring you to perform calculations, will ask you to consider qualitative and non-financial issues.

▶ Refer to MCQ cards (with Ch 1): 1 - 20 ◀

| Joint cost allocations | Make or buy decisions | Either/or problems | Shutdown decisions | Operational gearing |

Joint products

> Two or more products produced by the same process and separated in processing, each having a sufficiently high saleable value to merit recognition as a main product

Distinguishing features of joint products

- They are produced in the same process.
- They are indistinguishable from each other until the separation point.
- They each have a substantial sales value (after further processing, if necessary).
- They may require future processing after the separation point.

Apportioning joint/common costs

Costs incurred up to the point of separation (**split-off point**) need to be apportioned between the joint products for the purposes of stock valuation, profitability analysis and pricing.

> **Joint product costs are not used for decision making.**

There are four methods of doing this.

1: Physical measurement

- Cost is apportioned on the basis of the proportion that the output of each product bears by weight or volume to the total output.
- It is unsuitable where products separate during processing into different states.
- It ignores sales value and may lead to inappropriate results if sales values and volumes differ significantly.

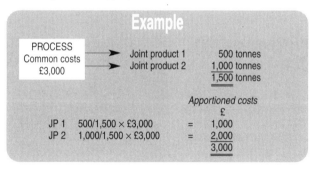

| Joint cost allocations | Make or buy decisions | Either/or problems | Shutdown decisions | Operational gearing |

2: Sales value at split-off point

Cost is apportioned according to products' ability to produce income (that is, in the proportions that the sales value of the products bear to the sales value of the process's total output).

Example

PROCESS
Common costs £3,000
→ Joint product 1 Sales value £5,000
→ Joint product 2 Sales value £10,000
                                £15,000

	£
JP 1 apportioned costs = 5,000/15,000 x £3,000 =	1,000
JP 2 apportioned costs = 10,000/15,000 x £3,000 =	2,000
	3,000

3: Sales value minus further processing costs

If the sales value at split-off point is not available, costs can be apportioned on the basis of residual / notional / proxy sales value (final sales value minus further processing costs).

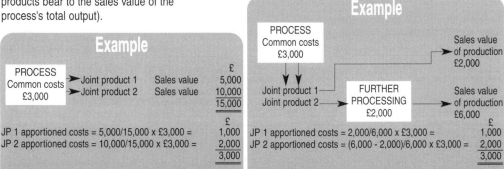

Example

PROCESS
Common costs £3,000
→ Joint product 1 → Sales value of production £2,000
→ Joint product 2 → FURTHER PROCESSING £2,000 → Sales value of production £6,000

	£
JP 1 apportioned costs = 2,000/6,000 x £3,000 =	1,000
JP 2 apportioned costs = (6,000 - 2,000)/6,000 x £3,000 =	2,000
	3,000

4: Weighted average method

If 'units' of joint product are not comparable in terms of physical resemblance or physical weight (gas, liquid, solid etc), common costs are apportioned on the basis of 'weighted units' (units of joint product × weighting factor).

Example

PROCESS Common costs £3,000	→ Joint product 1	Output = 2,000 kg	Weighting factor 3
	→ Joint product 2	Output = 1,000 litres	Weighting factor 6

	Units	Weighting	Weighted units		Apportioned cost £
JP 1	2,000	3	6,000	(6/12) × £3,000 =	1,500
JP 2	1,000	6	6,000	(6/12) × £3,000 =	1,500
			12,000		3,000

Joint cost allocations	Make or buy decisions	Either/or problems	Shutdown decisions	Operational gearing

Further processing decision

A product should be further processed if its sales revenue minus its further processing costs exceeds its sales revenue at the split-off point. The apportionment of joint processing costs is irrelevant to the decision.

By-products

A supplementary or secondary product (arising as the result of a process), the value of which is small relative to that of the principal product(s)

Possible accounting treatments of by-products

Do NOT allocate joint costs to a by-product.

- Add the net sales revenue from the by-product to sales revenue of the main product.
- Treat the sales revenue of the by-product as a separate incidental source of revenue ('other income').
- Deduct the sales revenue of the by-product from the cost of production/sales of the main product.
- Deduct the net realisable value of the by-product from the cost of production of the main product (most common method).

The choice of method will be influenced by the circumstances of production and ease of calculation, as much as by conceptual correctness. The method you are most likely to come across in examinations is the last method.

| Joint cost allocations | **Make or buy decisions** | Either/or problems | Shutdown decisions | Operational gearing |

No scarce resources

The relevant costs of the decision are the differential costs between making and buying.

Further considerations

- How to use freed up capacity
- Could using an outside supplier cause an industrial dispute?
- Subcontractor delivery reliability and product quality
- Loss of flexibility and control by subcontracting

With scarce resources

If an organisation has to subcontract because of insufficient in-house resources, total costs are minimised if those units bought have the lowest extra variable cost of buying (compared with making in-house) per unit of scarce resource saved by buying.

Example (limited labour time)

	A	B
Variable cost of making	£16	£14
Variable cost of buying	£20	£19
Extra variable cost of buying	£4	£5
Labour hours saved by buying	2	2
Extra variable cost of buying per hour saved	£2	£2.50
Priority for making in-house	2nd	1st

| Joint cost allocations | Make or buy decisions | **Either/or problems** | Shutdown decisions | Operational gearing |

The best approach is to draw up a three-column table with columns for the first option, for the second option and for the differences between the options.

- Do savings and costs separately and put one type in brackets. It doesn't matter which way round you do this as long as you are consistent within the question.
- Subtract column 2 from column 1, taking care with minus signs: $-50,000 - (-45,000) = -5,000$

Example

	Option 1	Option 2	Net (savings)/ costs
	£	£	£
Savings			
Saving 1	(500)	(100)	(400)
Saving 2	(300)	(600)	300
Costs			
Cost 1	0	200	(200)
Cost 2	700	0	700
Net cost			400

Conclusion. Option 1 costs £400 more than option 2. (Alternatively, option 2 would bring savings of £400 more than option 1.)

| Joint cost allocations | Make or buy decisions | Either/or problems | **Shutdown decisions** | Operational gearing |

Shutdown problems involve decisions about whether to close down a product line, department or other activity, perhaps because it is making losses or running costs are too expensive and if the decision is to shut down, whether the closure should be permanent or temporary.

Other considerations

In practice this sort of decision has long-term consequences.

- Is the closure to be a permanent reduction in capacity, and is this desirable?
- What is the impact on employees, customers, competitors and suppliers?

Financial considerations

The basic method is to use short-run relevant costs to calculate contributions and profits or losses.

1. Calculate what is earned by the process at present (perhaps in comparison with others).

2. Calculate what will be the financial consequences of closing down (selling machines, redundancy costs etc).

3. Compare the results and act accordingly.

4. Bear in mind that some fixed costs may no longer be incurred if the decision is to shut down and they are therefore relevant to the decision.

| Joint cost allocations | Make or buy decisions | Either/or problems | Shutdown decisions | **Operational gearing** |

Operational gearing / leverage

> The relationship of the fixed cost to the total cost of an operating unit

Operational gearing and risk

The greater the proportion of total costs that are fixed, the higher the operational gearing and hence the higher the level of risk (as any change in sales volume would have a greater impact on profit).

Operational gearing ratio → $\dfrac{\text{Contribution}}{\text{Profit}}$

Calculating change in profit due to change in sales volume

The following holds if cost and selling prices remain constant.

> **Change in profit = original profit × change in sales × operational gearing ratio**

Example

Contribution = £1,200,000 and fixed costs = £300,000
Sales volume increases by 25%

Operational gearing ratio = 1,200,000 ÷ 900,000 = 4/3

Change in profit = £(1,200,000 − 300,000) × 25% × 4/3
= £300,000

Revised profit = £(900,000 + 300,000) = £1,200,000

3: Quantitative techniques

Topic List

Risk and uncertainty

Probability

Decision trees

Value of information

Pareto analysis

Simulation models

This chapter covers some of the quantitative techniques that the management accountant can use when preparing information for management decisions. Topics covered here lend themselves particularly well to objective testing format.

> Key questions to try in the kit: 7, 8
> Refer to MCQ cards (with Ch 4): 21 - 34

| Risk and uncertainty | Probability | Decision trees | Value of information | Pareto analysis | Simulation models |

Risk

Involves situations or events which may or may not occur, but whose probability of occurrence can be calculated statistically and the frequency of their occurrence predicted from past records

Uncertainty

Involves events whose outcome *cannot* be predicted with statistical confidence

An event will be risky or uncertain depending on whether or not sufficient information is available to allow the lack of certainty to be quantified. As a rule, however, the terms are used interchangeably.

Attitude to risk

Risk seeker A decision maker interested in the best outcomes no matter how small the chance that they may occur

Risk neutral A decision maker concerned with what will be the most likely outcome

Risk averse A decision maker who acts on the assumption that the worst outcome might occur

The risk of a particular course of action should be considered in the context of the overall 'portfolio' of strategies adopted by an organisation.

Allowing for uncertainty

Method 1: Conservative estimates

Outcomes are estimated in a conservative manner in order to provide a built-in safety factor.

This method fails to give explicit consideration to a range of outcomes, however, and by concentrating only on conservative figures, it may also fail to consider the most likely outcomes.

Method 2: Three-point estimates

Data are provided for the most likely, for pessimistic and for optimistic outcomes, thus providing information on a range of possible outcomes.

Method 3: Sensitivity analysis

There are two useful approaches.

- Estimate by how much costs and revenues would need to differ from their estimated values before the decision would change.
- Estimate whether a decision would change if estimated costs were X% higher than anticipated, or estimated revenues Y% lower than anticipated.

The essence of the approach is to carry out calculations with one set of values and then substitute other possible values for the variables to see how this affects the overall outcome.

Sensitivity analysis is covered in more detail in Chapter 11 in the context of assessing the risk and uncertainty inherent in an investment project.

| Risk and uncertainty | **Probability** | Decision trees | Value of information | Pareto analysis | Simulation models |

Expected values (EV)

> The EV of an opportunity is equal to the sum of (the probability of an outcome occurring × the return expected if it does occur) = Σpx
> (where p = probability of an outcome occurring and x = value of that outcome).

The calculation of EVs is more useful as a decision-making technique when outcomes will occur many times over (for example, the calculation of expected sales levels on the basis of sales levels over 360 previous days) rather than when a decision must be made once only (such as an investment decision based on a 70% chance of a profit of £50,000 and a 30% chance of a loss of £70,000).

Example

If contribution could be £10,000, £20,000 or £30,000 with respective probabilities of 0.3, 0.5 and 0.2, the EV of contribution =

	£
£10,000 × 0.3	3,000
£20,000 × 0.5	10,000
£30,000 × 0.2	6,000
EV of contribution	19,000

There may be further additional conditions, for example there may be only a 75% chance of making one of these three positive contributions and a 25% chance of a negative contribution of £10,000, in which case the EV = (£19,000 (calculation above) × 0.75) – (£10,000 × 0.25) = £14,250 – £2,500 = £11,750.

Bayes' strategy

> When faced with a number of alternative decisions each with a range of possible outcomes, the optimum decision will be the one which gives the highest EV.

Cumulative probabilities

In the example opposite the cumulative probability that, say, total cost will be less than £10,000 is the sum of the combined probabilities for any total cost figure below £10,000 = 0.3 + 0.45 + 0.1 = 0.85.

Joint/combined probabilities

Example

If there is a 40% chance that costs will be £8 and a 75% probability that sales will be 500 units, the joint/combined probability of these two events is $0.4 \times 0.75 = 0.3$ and if other probabilities are £10 (60%) and 1,000 units (25%), the information can be tabulated as follows.

Volume	Prob	Cost	Prob	Combined prob	Total cost £	EV of total cost £
500	0.75	£8	0.4	0.30	4,000	1,200
		£10	0.6	0.45	5,000	2,250
1,000	0.25	£8	0.4	0.10	8,000	800
		£10	0.6	0.15	10,000	1,500
				1.00		5,750

Point estimate probabilities

A point estimate probability is the estimate of the probability of a particular outcome occurring.

Example

Point estimate probabilities for variable cost per unit might be £19.50, £19.70 and £20.10 but, in reality, the actual variable cost per unit might be any amount from below £19.50 to above £20.10.

Advantages

- The provide some estimate of risk.
- If there are enough point estimates, they can be a reasonable approximation of a continuous probability distribution.
- They can be assumed to represent a range of values.

Disadvantages

- They can be unrealistic.
- They are only an approximation of the risks/uncertainty in estimates.
- They may give the impression that they are the only possible outcomes.

| Risk and uncertainty | Probability | **Decision trees** | Value of information | Pareto analysis | Simulation models |

Preparation

1 Start with a (labelled) **decision point**.

2 Add branches for each option/alternative.

3 If the outcome of an option is 100% certain, the branch for that alternative is complete.

4 If the outcome of an option is uncertain (because they are a number of possible outcomes), add an **outcome point**.

5 For each possible outcome, add a branch (with the relevant probability) to the outcome point.

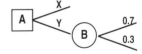

6 Always work **chronologically** from **left to right**.

| Risk and uncertainty | Probability | **Decision trees** | Value of information | Pareto analysis | Simulation models |

Evaluating the decision

Work from **right to left** and calculate the EV of revenue/cost/contribution/profit at each outcome point (**rollback analysis**).

Example

As a result of an increase in demand for a town's car parking facilities, the owners of a car park are reviewing their business operations. A decision has to be made now to select one of the following three options for the next year.

Option 1: Make no change. Annual profit is £100,000. There is little likelihood that this will provoke new competition this year.

Option 2: Raise prices by 50%. If this occurs there is a 75% chance that an entrepreneur will set up in competition this year. The Board's estimate of its annual profit in this situation would be as follows.

2A WITH a new competitor		2B WITHOUT a new competitor	
Probability	Profit	Probability	Profit
0.3	£150,000	0.7	£200,000
0.7	£120,000	0.3	£150,000

Option 3: Expand the car park quickly, at a cost of £50,000, keeping prices the same. The profits are then estimated to be like 2B above, except that the probabilities would be 0.6 and 0.4 respectively.

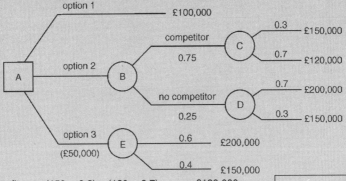

At C, expected profit = $(150 \times 0.3) + (120 \times 0.7)$ = £129,000
At D, expected profit = $(200 \times 0.7) + (150 \times 0.3)$ = £185,000
At B, expected profit = $(129 \times 0.75) + (185 \times 0.25)$ = £143,000
At E, expected profit = $(200 \times 0.6) + (150 \times 0.4)$ = £180,000

Option	Expected profit £'000
1	100
2	143
3 (180 – 50)	130

| Risk and uncertainty | Probability | Decision trees | **Value of information** | Pareto analysis | Simulation models |

The value of perfect information

1. Work out the EVs of all options and see which is best.

2. See what decision would be taken with perfect information (if all the outcomes were known in advance with certainty) and calculate the EV.

3. The value of the information (the amount one should be willing to pay to obtain it)
= EV of the action you would take *with* the information – EV without the information.

Alternatively a decision tree can be used.

Example

	Profit if strong demand	Profit/(loss) if weak demand
Option A	£4,000	£(1,000)
Option B	£1,500	£600
Probability	0.3	0.7

EV of A = $4,000 \times 0.3 + (1,000) \times 0.7$ = £500
EV of B = $1,500 \times 0.3 + 600 \times 0.7$ = £870

∴ Choose B

With perfect information, if demand is strong choose A but if demand is weak choose B.

∴ EV with perfect information = $0.3 \times 4,000 + 0.7 \times 600$
= £1,620

∴ Value of perfect information = £(1,620 – 870)
= £750

The value of imperfect information

The calculation of the value of imperfect information requires the use of **posterior probabilities**. These can be established by drawing a decision tree or using Bayes' theorem, but the safest way is to use tabulation (see the example which follows).

If you do decide to use Bayes' theorem, you need to remember:

$$P(B/A) = \frac{P(A \text{ and } B)}{P(A)} = \frac{P(B)P(A/B)}{P(A)}$$

Once calculated, the probabilities can be inserted on the branches of a decision tree and EVs calculated using rollback analysis.

> If the examiner asks you to calculate the maximum amount that should be paid for a forecast you need to calculate the value of imperfect information!

> To date this topic has only been examined once, in Section A.

| Risk and uncertainty | Probability | Decision trees | **Value of information** | Pareto analysis | Simulation models |

Example

X Ltd is trying to decide whether or not to build a shopping centre. The probability that the centre will be successful based on past experience is 0.6.

X Ltd could conduct market research to help with the decision.

- If the centre is going to be successful there is a 75% chance that the market research will say so.
- If the centre is not going to be successful there is a 95% chance that the survey will say so.

The information can be tabulated as follows.

		Actual Success	Failure	Total	
Research	Success	** 45	2	47	* given
	Failure	*** 15	38	53	** 0.75 × 60
Total		* 60	40	100	*** balancing figure

The probabilities are as follows.

P (research says success) = 0.47
P (research says failure) = 0.53

If the survey says success

P (success) = 45/47 = 0.957
P (failure) = 2/47 = 0.043

If the survey says failure

P (success) = 15/53 = 0.283
P (failure) = 38/53 = 0.717

The value of imperfect information = difference between (EV if open shopping centre without performing market research) and (EV if conduct market research and then decide whether or not to open the shopping centre).

| Risk and uncertainty | Probability | Decision trees | Value of information | **Pareto analysis** | Simulation models |

Pareto analysis

This basically means finding out what proportion of a total is represented by each of the individual things making up the total. For example, here is a Pareto analysis of sales.

Example (for sales)

Product	Sales Units	Sales %	Cumulative sales Units	Cumulative sales %
A	1,000	43	1,000	43
B	800	35	1,800	78
C	500	22	2,300	100
	2,300	100		

A similar analysis could be done for any other aspect of product data: contribution, cost, complaints or whatever.

Using Pareto analysis

You might have to do a Pareto analysis of sales levels as compared with contribution or amount of stock held.

Typically this reveals that the products/divisions that sell the most are different from the products/divisions that provide the highest contribution or have the highest levels of stocks.

This may suggest management action such as the revision of pricing policy or the discontinuance of certain products.

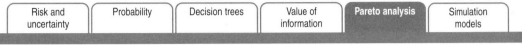

80/20 rule

Strictly speaking 'Pareto' is synonymous with the 80/20 rule - 80% of something is accounted for by 20% of something else (for example 80% of stock value is represented by only 20% of stock items).

This should not be interpreted too literally - the basic principle is that a few items or activities are often core to an organisation's fortunes while the majority are only peripheral.

Example

If an organisation uses ABC, a pareto analysis of cost drivers might show that, say, 15% of cost drivers are responsible for 80% of total cost.

Diagrammatic representation: 1

Diagrammatic representation: 2

Pareto analysis

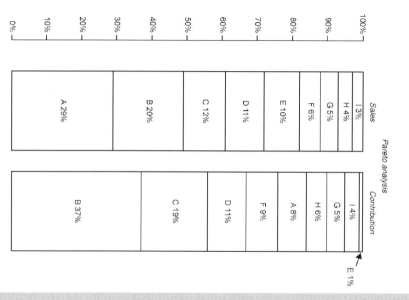

Sales: A 29% | B 20% | C 12% | D 11% | E 10% | F 6% | G 5% | H 4% | I 3%

Contribution: B 37% | C 19% | D 11% | F 9% | A 8% | H 6% | G 5% | I 4% | E 1%

| Risk and uncertainty | Probability | Decision trees | Value of information | Pareto analysis | **Simulation models** |

Monte Carlo method

1. Identify the probabilities of particular variable values occurring.

2. Allocate a range of numbers to each possible variable value in proportion to the probabilities.

    - Probability to 1 decimal place → 10 numbers (0-9), probability to 2 decimal places → 100 numbers (00-99) and so on

    - A probability of 0.15 gets 0.15 of the total numbers to be assigned, that is 15 numbers: (00, 01, 02, 03, ..., 14)

3. Run the simulation model so that random numbers are generated (either manually or by a computer).

4. Allocate variable values on the basis of the generated random numbers.

Example

Daily demand	Probability	Numbers assigned
Units		
17	0.15	00-14
18	0.45	15-59
19	0.40	60-99
	1.00	

Random numbers for a simulation over three days are 761301.

Day	Random number	Demand
1	76	19
2	13	17
3	01	17

4: Linear programming (simplex)

Topic List

Formulating the problem

Interpretation of the final tableau

Sensitivity analysis

Using linear programming

The simplex method is a method of solving linear programming problems with two or more decision variables. It is new to the Paper 9 syllabus (having previously been in the Paper 8 syllabus).

> Key question to try in the kit: 15
> Refer to MCQ cards (with Ch 3): 21 - 34

| Formulating the problem | Interpretation of the final tableau | Sensitivity analysis | Using linear programming |

Six steps to formulating the problem

1 Define variables

Let x = number of product X produced each month

Let y = number of product Y produced each month

2 Establish objective function

For example, maximise contribution (C) = $20x + 16y$ subject to the following constraints.

3 Establish constraints

For example:

Materials	$5x + 2y \leq 3{,}000$
Labour	$x + 3y \leq 1{,}750$
Machine time	$3x + 2y \leq 2{,}100$
Non negativity	

> In the exam you need to be able to formulate the problem and interpret the final tableau.

4 Introduce slack variables

> A slack variable represents the amount of a constraining resource or item that is unused. One is required for each non-negativity constraint.

Let a = quantity of unused materials
b = number of unused labour hours
c = number of unused machine hours

The slack variables a, b, c will be equal to 0 in the final solution only if the combined production of x and y uses up all the available materials, labour and machine time.

5 Redefine constraints

$5x + 2y + a = 3,000$
$x + 3y + b = 1,750$
$3x + 2y + c = 2,100$

6 Redefine objective function

- Express it as an equation with the right hand side equal to zero.
- Insert the slack variables but with zero coefficients

Maximise contribution (C) given by $C - 20x - 16y + 0a + 0b + 0c = 0$

| Formulating the problem | **Interpretation of the final tableau** | Sensitivity analysis | Using linear programming |

Here is the optimal solution for the example detailed in Steps 1 to 6.

Example

Variables in solution	x	y	a	b	c	Solution column
x	1	0	0	−0.29	0.43	400
a	0	0	1	0.59	−1.87	100
y	0	1	0	0.43	−0.14	450
Solution row	0	0	0	1.08	6.36	15,200

- The solution is optimal because the shadow prices in the bottom row are all positive.
- Make and sell 400 units of X and 450 of Y to earn contribution of £15,200.
- 100 units of material will be unused.
- All labour and machine time will be used.
- The shadow price of labour time (b) is £1.08 (the amount by which contribution would increase if more labour time could be made available at its normal variable cost).
- The shadow price of materials is nil.

| Formulating the problem | Interpretation of the final tableau | **Sensitivity analysis** | Using linear programming |

Look back at the final tableau on page 36.

Having more or less of a scarce resource

The figures in the (b) column provide the following information for each extra labour hour that is available.

- Contribution would increase by £1.08.
- 0.29 units less of X would be made, losing contribution of 0.29 × 20 = £5.80.
- The value of (a) unused materials would increase by 0.59 units.
- 0.43 units more of Y would be made, increasing contribution by 0.43 × 16 = £6.88.

- The net increase in contribution = £(6.88 − 5.80) = £1.08.
- The limit to the number of extra labour hours that would earn an extra £1.08 = 400 (x in the optimal tableau) ÷ 0.29 (the reduction in x for each extra labour hour)) = 1,379.3 hours, so that the shadow price is only valid up to a total limit of 1,750 + 1,379.3 = 3,129.3 hours.

Obtaining extra resources at a premium on cost

It would not be worth obtaining extra labour via overtime working at time and a half (say £2 per hour premium) as this is greater than the extra contribution of £1.08 per hour.

| Formulating the problem | Interpretation of the final tableau | **Sensitivity analysis** | Using linear programming |

Using computer packages

Typical output from a computer package

Objective function (c)			
		270,000	— Total optimal contribution is £270,000.
Variable	Value	Relative loss	
x	20	0.00	
y	130	0.00	— If one unit of Z were made, total contribution would fall by £75.
z	0	75.00	
Constraint	Slack/surplus	Worth	— Slack = 90 means 90 units of resource 1 unused.
1 ($\leq$)	90.00	0.00	— Slack = 0 means all resource 2 is used. Contribution would increase by £50 for each unit of resource 2 made available.
2 ($\leq$)	0.00	50.00	
3 (limit on y)	0.00	250.00	— Slack = 0 means limit has been met. Contribution would increase by £250 if the limit on Y could be raised by 1.
4 (minimum X (1))	19.00	0.00	— Surplus = 19 means (19 + 1) units of X made.

Interpretation

To maximise contribution produce 20 units of X and 130 units of Y.

- In general any constraint with a slack of zero has a positive worth figure, while any constraint with a positive slack figure will have a worth of zero.
- In general, only those decision variables with a relative loss of zero will have a positive value in the optimal solution.

A question in the November 2001 exam (Paper 8) contained output from a computer package for linear programming similar to that below.

Variables

| A | 50 |
| B | 30 |

Constraints

N1	3,000	
N2		5
N3		4

Contribution £100,000

To check the meaning of the figures, you could calculate the usage of resource N1 given production of 50 A and 30 B. If the difference between availability and usage of N1 is 3000, you would then know that £5 and £4 were shadow prices.

| Formulating the problem | Interpretation of the final tableau | Sensitivity analysis | **Using linear programming** |

Further assumptions (in addition to those which apply to limiting factor analysis (Paper 8))

- The total amount of each scare resource is known with certainty.
- There is no interdependence between the demand for different products.

Uses

- Selling different products
- Calculation of relevant costs
- Maximum payment for additional scarce resources
- Budgeting
- Control
- Capital budgeting

Practical difficulties

- The identification of resources in short supply and their availability is problematic.
- Management may opt for a 'satisfactory' product mix rather than one that is profit maximising.
- The assumption of linearity may be totally invalid. For example the learning effect may be relevant.
- The model is essential static.
- Variables can only take on integer values.
- The shadow price only applies up to a certain limit.

5: Pricing

Topic List

- Demand
- Influences
- Optimal pricing
- Cost-based approaches
- Strategies
- Variances

Historically, price setting was the single most important decision made by the sales department and the typical reaction was to cut prices in order to sell more. Modern businesses, however, seek to interpret and satisfy customer wants and needs by modifying existing products or introducing new ones.

Not withstanding this 'change' in emphasis, pricing is still very important, in terms of profitability, survival and as a competitive tool.

> Key questions to try in the kit: 17, 19, 20
> Refer to MCQ cards: 35 - 54

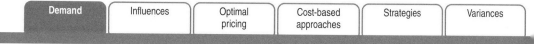

Price elasticity of demand (η)

A measure of the extent of change in market demand for a good, in response to a change in its price

= change in quantity demanded, as a % of demand / change in price, as a % of price

Inelastic demand

- $\eta < 1$
- Steep demand curve
- Demand falls by a smaller % than % rise in price
- Pricing decision: increase prices

Elastic demand

- $\eta > 1$
- Shallow demand curve
- Demand falls by a larger % than % rise in price
- Pricing decision: decide whether change in cost will be less than change in revenue

Degrees of elasticity

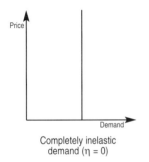

Completely inelastic demand ($\eta = 0$)

Demand is totally unresponsive to changes in price.

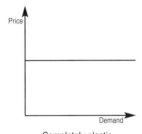

Completely elastic demand ($\eta = \infty$)

Demand is limitless at price P but non-existent above price P.

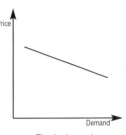

Elastic demand

The 'normal' situation, demand increasing as prices are lowered.

| Demand | Influences | Optimal pricing | Cost-based approaches | Strategies | Variances |

Factors determining the degree of elasticity

- The price of the good
- The price of other goods
- The size and distribution of household incomes
- Tastes and fashion
- Expectations
- Obsolescence

Other elasticities

- **Income elasticity**

  $$\frac{\% \text{ change in quantity demanded}}{\% \text{ change in income}}$$

- **Cross elasticity**

  $$\frac{\% \text{ change in quantity demanded of X}}{\% \text{ change in price of Y}}$$

Demand and the individual firm

The volume of demand for one organisation's goods rather than another's is influenced by three principal factors.

1 **Product life cycle (PLC)**

- Introduction – potential customers unaware of product, advertising needed
- Growth – demand increases
- Maturity – modifications/improvements to sustain demand
- Decline – market will have bought enough of the product

2 **Quality** – the better the quality, the greater the demand

3 **Marketing (4 Ps)**

- Price
- Product
- Place – potential buyers will turn to substitutes if a good is difficult to obtain
- Promotion – brand names, shop displays and free gifts will stimulate demand

Markets

The price that an organisation can charge will be determined to some degree by the market in which it operates.

- Perfect competition
- Monopolistic competition
- Monopoly
- Oligopoly

Competition

How to fight a price war

- Sell on value, not on price
- Target service
- Use 'package pricing'
- Make price comparisons difficult
- Build up key accounts
- Explore new pricing models

Other factors which influence price

- Price sensitivity of purchasers (eg business traveller considers level of service rather than price)
- Price perception (eg designer labels)
- Compatibility with other products
- Competitors' actions and reactions
- Suppliers' prices
- Inflation
- Quality connotations
- Income effects (eg during a recession)
- Substitute products
- Ethics

| Demand | Influences | **Optimal pricing** | Cost-based approaches | Strategies | Variances |

Deriving the demand curve

If demand is linear the equation for the demand curve is

$$P = a - \frac{bQ}{\Delta Q}$$

where P = price

Q = quantity demanded

a = price at which demand would be nil

b = amount by which price rises for each stepped change in demand

ΔQ = stepped change (decrease) in demand

Example

$P = £10$
$Q = 100$ units
Q falls to 95 units if P rises to £11.

$a = £10 + ((100/5) \times 1) = £30$

$P = 30 - Q/5$

$$a = £(\text{current price}) + \left(\frac{\text{current quantity at current price}}{\text{change in quantity when price changed by } £b} \times £b \right)$$

| Demand | Influences | **Optimal pricing** | Cost-based approaches | Strategies | Variances |

Example: without using the demand curve formula

Maximum demand for LM Ltd's product is 7,000 units per annum.
Demand will reduce by 150 units for every £1 increase in the selling price.

∴ When p = 0, demand (x) = 7,000
When p = 1, demand (x) = 6,850

∴ Demand (x) = 7,000 − 150p, where p is the selling price in £
(because demand will drop by 150 units for every increase (from £0) of £1 in the selling price)

If the profit-maximising annual sales level is, say, 4,000 units, the profit-maximising selling price can be calculated.

x = 7,000 − 150p
If x = 4,000, p = £20

Determining the profit-maximising selling price/output level

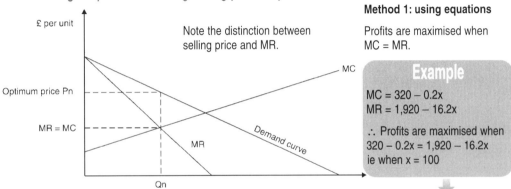

Note the distinction between selling price and MR.

Method 1: using equations

Profits are maximised when MC = MR.

Example

$MC = 320 - 0.2x$
$MR = 1{,}920 - 16.2x$

∴ Profits are maximised when
$320 - 0.2x = 1{,}920 - 16.2x$
ie when $x = 100$

You could also be provided with/asked to determine the demand curve in order to calculate the price at this profit-maximising output level.

| Demand | Influences | **Optimal pricing** | Cost-based approaches | Strategies | Variances |

Method 2: visual inspection of tabulation of data

1 Work out the demand curve and hence the price and total revenue (PQ) at various levels of demand.

2 Calculate total cost and hence marginal cost at each level of demand.

3 Calculate profit at each level of demand, thereby determining the price and level of demand that maximises profit.

Method 4: using gradients

At the point of profit maximisation, gradients of the total cost and total revenue curves are equal.

Method 3: graphical approach

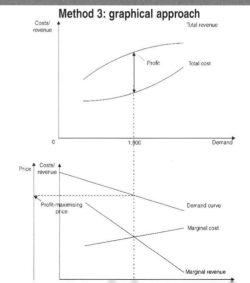

| Demand | Influences | Optimal pricing | **Cost-based approaches** | Strategies | Variances |

Full cost plus pricing

The sales price is determined by calculating the full cost of the product and then adding a % mark-up for profit.

- An average profit mark-up can be used as a general guideline if prices must be quoted regularly to prospective customers.
- The mark-up does not have to be rigid and fixed but can be varied to suit the circumstances.

Problems

- The price must be adjusted to suit market and demand conditions.
- Output volume (a key factor in the determination of the overhead absorption rate) has to be budgeted.
- Suitable overhead absorption bases must be selected.
- Most importantly, full cost plus pricing fails to recognise that since demand may be determined by price, there will be a profit-maximising combination of price and demand.

A full cost determined by activity based costing as opposed to absorption costing might be more appropriate in today's business environment.

| Demand | Influences | Optimal pricing | **Cost-based approaches** | Strategies | Variances |

Marginal cost plus pricing / mark-up pricing

> Sales price = marginal cost of production (or marginal cost of sales) + profit margin

Pricing in a limiting factor situation

Suppose a business is working at full capacity and is restricted by a shortage of resources from expanding its output further. By deciding what target profit it would like to earn, it can establish a mark-up per unit of limiting factor.

Advantages of mark-up pricing

- ☑ Simple and easy
- ☑ Mark-up percentage can be varied to reflect demand conditions
- ☑ Helps create a better awareness of the concepts and implications of marginal cost and CVP analysis
- ☑ Used by businesses where there is a readily-identifiable basic variable cost (eg retail industries)

Drawbacks of mark-up pricing

- ☒ Does not ensure that sufficient attention is paid to demand conditions, competitors' prices and profit maximisation
- ☒ Ignores fixed overheads

| Demand | Influences | Optimal pricing | Cost-based approaches | **Strategies** | Variances |

Product bundling

Sell a number of products/services as a package at a price lower than the sum of their individual prices (eg hotel package includes use of leisure facilities).

Psychological pricing

Price a product at £9.99 instead of £10 or withdraw an unsuccessful product from the market and relaunch it at a higher price (customers perceiving lower price = lower quality).

Premium pricing

Make a product appear different to justify a premium price.

Multiple products and loss leaders

Charge a very low price for one product to make consumers buy additional products in the range which carry higher margins.

New products

If the product is the first of its kind, use market research to find out what customers are willing to pay.

Special orders

Use **minimum pricing** to price special orders (which arise if an organisation has spare capacity or it has no regular source of income and relies exclusively on its ability to respond to demand (eg building firm)).

Market penetration pricing

A policy of low prices when a product is first introduced in order to obtain sufficient penetration in the market

When to use

- To discourage new entrants into the market
- To shorten the initial period of the PLC
- If demand is highly elastic
- If significant economies of scale are possible with high output volumes

Market skimming

A policy of charging high prices when a product is first launched, and lower prices as it moves into later stages of the PLC

When to use

- If a product is new and different
- If strength of demand and price sensitivity are unknown
- If product differentiation is possible
- To make a quick profit if the PLC is short

Differential pricing and price discrimination

In certain circumstances an organisation can charge some customers more than others because some are willing to pay more for the same product/service.

Bases on which discriminating prices can be set

- By market segment (eg lower priced cinema seats for students)
- By product version (eg 'add on extras' in car models)
- By place (eg theatre seats)
- By time (eg off-peak travel bargains)

Pricing to recover an investment

This is based on achieving a minimum payback period.

When to use

- If the business is high risk
- If rapid changes in fashion/technology are expected
- If an innovator is short of cash

Splitting the sales volume variance

The overall sales volume variance can be split into sales mix and quantity variances, or market size and market share variances.

The sales mix and quantity variances are only meaningful where management can control the proportions of the products sold (through allocation of advertising expenses, sales effort and so on).

Sales mix variance

- Occurs when the proportions of the various products sold are different from those budgeted
- Calculated as the difference between what the mix of products actually sold should have been, and what it was, valued at the standard margin per unit

Example

Convert actual total sales (say 500 units) into budgeted mix (say 3:2)

	Product A	Product B
Mix should have been	300 units	200 units
but was (say)	200 units	300 units
Mix variance in units	100 units (A)	100 units (F)
× std margin per unit (say)	× £10	× £5
Mix variance in £	£1,000 (A)	£500 (F)
Total mix variance in £		£500 (A)

Sales quantity variance

- Shows the difference in contribution/profit caused by a difference between the budgeted and actual sales volumes
- Calculated as the difference between the budgeted sales volumes and the actual total sales volume in the budgeted proportions, multiplied by the standard margin per unit

Example

	Product A	Product B
Actual sales in budgeted mix (as above)	300 units	200 units
Budgeted sales (say)	360 units	240 units
Quantity variance in units	60 units (A)	40 units (A)
× std margin per unit	× £10	× £5
Quantity variance in £	£600 (A)	£200 (A)
Total quantity variance in £		£800 (A)

The mix and quantity variances are usually valued at standard margin but they could be valued at standard selling price. They could not then be used to perform a full profit reconciliation, however, but they could be used to evaluate the impact on sales value of a change in volume.

Market size variance

- Indicates the change in margin/contribution caused by a change in the size of the market
- Could be identified as a planning variance

Example

Revised sales volume, given industry sales	X units
Original budgeted sales volume	X units
Variance in units	X units
× standard margin/contribution per unit **OR** weighted average std selling price	× £X
Market size variance	£X

Market share variance

- Indicates the change in margin/contribution caused by a change in the market share achieved
- Could be identified as an operational variance

Example

Actual sales volume	X units
Revised sales volume, given industry sales	X units
Variance in units	X units
× standard margin/contribution per unit **OR** weighted average std selling price	× £X
Market share variance	£X

MCQs in past exams have entailed valuing the variances using **weighted average standard selling price** and **contribution per unit** bases.

6: Transfer pricing

Topic List

The aims of transfer pricing

General rules

Setting transfer prices

Negotiated transfer prices and subsidies

Multinational transfer pricing

Beware of getting too bogged down in the mathematical and mechanical aspects of transfer pricing: make sure that you can describe the method required and explain the reasons why it is suitable.

Look out for both MCQs and long questions on this topic.

Key questions to try in the kit: 26, 28, 30
Refer to MCQ cards: 55 - 65

| The aims of transfer pricing | General rules | Setting transfer prices | Negotiated transfer prices and subsidies | Multinational transfer pricing |

Aim	How
Maintain the right level of divisional autonomy	Transfer prices must be set to provide incentive and motivation, although head office authority will be required to ensure goal congruence and prevent dysfunctional decision making.
Ensure divisional performance is measured fairly	Transfer prices must be established at a fair commercial price to ensure appropriate behavioural decisions by divisional managers.
Ensure corporate profits are maximised	The transfer price should encourage divisional managers to agree on the amount of goods transferred, which will also be at a level which is consistent with overall organisational aims such as maximising company profit.

Correctly-set transfer prices are therefore a way of promoting divisional autonomy, ideally without prejudicing the measurement of divisional performance or discouraging overall corporate profit maximisation.

| The aims of transfer pricing | **General rules** | Setting transfer prices | Negotiated transfer prices and subsidies | Multinational transfer pricing |

Limits within which transfer prices should fall

- **The minimum.** The sum of the supplying division's marginal cost and the opportunity cost of the item transferred
- **The maximum.** The lowest market price at which the receiving division could purchase the goods or services externally, less any internal cost savings in packaging and delivery

Example

Division A produces product D at a marginal cost of £350. If a unit is transferred internally to division B, £70 contribution is lost on an external sale. The item can be purchased externaly for £480.

- **Minimum.** Division A's minimum would be £(350 + 70) = £420
- **Maximum.** Division B's maximum would be £480

Savings from producing internally rather than buying externally = £60.

Opportunity cost

The opportunity cost included in determining the lower limit will be one of the following.

- Maximum contribution foregone by the supplying division in transferring internally rather than selling externally
- Contribution foregone by not using the same facilities for their next best alternative use

If there is **no external market** and no alternative uses for the facilities, **transfer price = standard variable cost of production**.

If there **is an external market** and no alternative uses for the facilities, **transfer price = market price**.

6: Transfer pricing

| The aims of transfer pricing | General rules | **Setting transfer prices** | Negotiated transfer prices and subsidies | Multinational transfer pricing |

Transfer prices based on market price

What is the ideal transfer price where a perfect external market exists? External market price
or
external market price less savings in selling costs

This applies whether or not variable costs and selling prices are constant.

Merits

Divisional autonomy. If profit centre managers are given freedom to negotiate prices with each other as though they were independent companies, market-based transfer prices will tend to result.

Divisional performance. Where a market price exists but the transfer price is a different amount, divisional managers will argue about the volume of internal transfers.

Corporate profit maximisation. Such an approach results in decisions which are in the best interests of the organisation as a whole.

Transfer prices based on cost – constant unit variable costs and selling prices

If there is an **imperfect external market**, the transfer price has to be based on cost.

1 Standard or actual? The use of standard costs is fairer because if actual costs are used the supplying division has no incentive to control its costs – it can pass on its inefficiencies to the receiving division.

2 Variable cost? The supplying division does not cover its fixed costs (although this problem can be overcome by some form of **dual pricing** or **two-part tariff** system).

3 Full cost? The supplying division makes no profit. And, as the transfer price increases, its effect on the receiving division could lead to organisational sub-optimisation problems.

4 Full cost plus? What margin will all parties perceive as fair?

If there is **no external market** for the item being transferred:

> **Goal congruent decisions will be made if the transfer price is ≥ variable cost in the supplying division but ≤ net marginal revenue in the receiving division.**

| The aims of transfer pricing | General rules | **Setting transfer prices** | Negotiated transfer prices and subsidies | Multinational transfer pricing |

Transfer prices based on cost – changing unit variable costs and selling prices

When unit variable costs and/or unit selling prices are not constant there will be a profit-maximising level of output and the ideal transfer price will only be found by careful analysis and sensible negotiation.

1 The starting point should be to establish the output and sales quantities that will optimise the profits of the company or group as a whole.

2 The next step is to establish the transfer price at which both the supplying division and the receiving division would maximise their profits at this company-optimising output level.

> **Divisional and organisational profits will be maximised if the transfer price is ≥ marginal cost in the supplying division but ≤ net marginal revenue in the receiving division**

Capacity constraints

If there is a capacity constraint resulting in a shortage of supplies of the product, the only way to be sure that a profit-maximising transfer price will be implemented is to dictate the policy from the centre.

| The aims of transfer pricing | General rules | Setting transfer prices | **Negotiated transfer prices and subsidies** | Multinational transfer pricing |

Negotiated transfer prices

When authority is decentralised to the extent that divisional managers negotiate transfer prices with each other, the agreed price may be finalised from a mixture of accounting arithmetic, politics and compromise.

Possibility 1: Market value minus reduction to allow for internal nature of the transaction

Possibility 2: For a near-finished product, market value of the end product minus an amount for finishing work

Disputes about transfer prices are likely to arise, however, and head office may either impose a price which maximises company profits or may ensure negotiations continue until a transfer price is agreed

---

More imposition by head office of its own decisions on divisions

⬇

Less decentralisation of authority

⬇

Less effective the profit centre system of accounting for motivating divisional managers

---

Using subsidies to spread risk

Suppose a large division requires a small division to supply components. Substantial investment and commitment to fixed cost expenditure would represent substantial risk to the small division.

The risk could be spread if the larger division were willing to contribute towards the fixed costs in return for a reduction in the transfer price.

| The aims of transfer pricing | General rules | Setting transfer prices | Negotiated transfer prices | **Multinational transfer pricing** |

Factors affecting transfer prices in multinationals	Comment
Exchange rate fluctuations	The value of transfers is affected.
Taxation in different countries	Manipulation of profits is possible by raising/lowering transfer prices.
Import tariffs	It is possible to minimise costs by minimising transfer prices.
Exchange controls	Restrictions on the transfer of profits can be overcome if head office provides goods/services to the subsidiary and charges exorbitantly high prices.
Anti-dumping legislation	A government might insist on fair market value as a transfer price.
Competitive pressures	Transfer pricing can be used to enable divisions to match/undercut local competitors.
Repatriation of funds	By inflating transfer prices for goods sold to divisions in countries with high inflation, these divisions' profits are reduced and funds are repatriated, saving their value.

Transfer pricing is often abused by multinational organisations to evade tax payments

7: Relating costs to cost objects

Topic List

Activity based costing (ABC)

Customer profitability analysis (CPA)

Direct product profitability (DPP)

Activity based management (ABM)

Behavioural aspects

As its title suggests, this chapter looks at various ways in which costs can be related to different cost objects (products, customers and so on) in different environments.

Key questions to try in the kit: 34, 35, 36
Refer to MCQ cards (with Chs 8 & 9):
66 - 109

| **Activity based costing (ABC)** | Customer profitability analysis (CPA) | Direct product profitability (DPP) | Activity based management (ABM) | Behavioural aspects |

Cost analysis in the modern business environment

Short-term variable costs that vary with production volume

Long-term variable costs (often costs of support activities) that vary according to the range and complexity of production

Volume versus variety

The problem of producing a small number of products in volume compared with producing a large variety of products in small runs

The modern philosophy of manufacturing in variety leads to an increase in the costs of support services.

Cost control requires that costs of support activities are related to products via their casual factors.

The ABC approach is to relate the cost of support activities to cost drivers

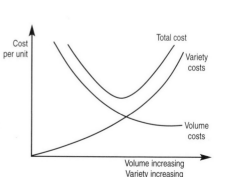

Cost drivers

> Any factor which causes a change in the cost of an activity

For long-term variable costs

These are related to the transactions/activities undertaken in support departments where the costs are incurred.

∴ Cost driver = transaction/activity in support department

For short-term variable costs

Cost driver = volume of activity (eg labour hrs)

Manufacturing cost hierarchy of activities

- Unit level (eg inspection of every nth item produced)
- Batch level (eg machine set-up costs)
- Product level (eg product advertising)
- Facility level (eg rates)

Types of transaction

- Logistical - organise flow of resources
- Balancing - ensure demand and supply of resources are matched
- Quality - ensure production is at the required quality level
- Change - ensure customers' requirements are met

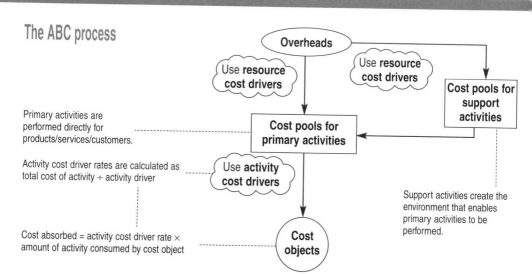

Merits of ABC

- Absorption costing tends to allocate too great a proportion of overheads to high-volume products (which cause relatively little diversity) and too small a proportion to low-volume products (which cause greater diversity and use more support services), whereas ABC traces a more appropriate amount. This has implications for pricing.
- Ideally suited to CPA and can be used in service organisations
- Help with cost reduction
- Takes product costing beyond traditional factory floor boundaries and considers overhead functions, such as product design and quality control

Criticisms of ABC

- More complex than absorption costing and so should only be introduced if it will provide additional management information
- Tends to burden low-volume (new) products with a punitive level of overhead and so could threaten innovation
- Can one cost driver explain the behaviour of all the items in a cost pool?
- Some measure of arbitrary cost apportionment needed for costs such as rent and rates
- Do decisions or the passage of time cause costs rather than activities? Or is there no clear cause of cost?

| Activity based costing (ABC) | **Customer profitability analysis (CPA)** | Direct product profitability (DPP) | Activity based management (ABM) | Behavioural aspects |

Customer profitability analysis (CPA)

The analysis of the revenues and costs associated with specific customers or customer groups

The relative profitability of specific customers/customer groups can be assessed, and strategies aimed at attracting and retaining the most profitable customers implemented.

Customers can be categorised using this grid.

- The aim is to attract as many accepting customers as possible.
- Many large retail organisations fall into the demanding category.

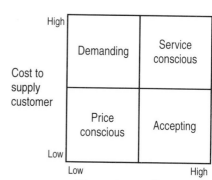

CPA and ABC

The necessary analysis of costs can be successfully carried out using ABC cost drivers.

> **Examples**
>
> | Cost | Cost driver |
> |---|---|
> | Delivery | Miles travelled |
> | After sales service and support | Number of visits |

CPA and Pareto's rule

Pareto's rule is often found to apply (20% of customers generate approximately 80% of total margin).

Customer life cycles

Customers can be costed over their life cycle and expected future cash flows discounted.

Customer profitability statement

> **Example**
>
> | | £'000 | £'000 |
> |---|---|---|
> | Revenue at list prices | | X |
> | Less: discounts given | | X |
> | Net revenue | | X |
> | Less: cost of goods sold | | X |
> | Gross margin | | X |
> | Less: customer specific costs | | X |
> | Less: financing costs | | |
> | credit period | X | |
> | customer specific inventory | X | |
> | | | X |
> | Net margin from customer | | X |

| Activity based costing (ABC) | Customer profitability analysis (CPA) | **Direct product profitability (DPP)** | Activity based management (ABM) | Behavioural aspects |

DPP

A costing system used primarily within the retail sector. It involves the attribution of costs other than purchase price (eg warehousing) to each product line. A net profit, as opposed to a gross profit, can therefore be identified for each product.

Make sure you do the pilot paper question (Question 41 in the Kit) on this topic.

Why is DPP important?

- Gross profit includes none of the organisation's own costs and so provides little planning and control information.
- Some product categories consume more of the organisation's resources than others (eg storage) and so an attempt to relate these direct costs to products is needed.

Direct product costs and profit

Direct product profit is the contribution a product category makes to fixed costs and profits.

Sales price
- Purchase price

Gross margin
+ Other direct revenues
- Direct product costs

Direct product profit

- Only occur occasionally (eg if the retailer receives a discount from the manufacturer for point of sale promotion)

Direct product costs can be directly attributed to the handling and storing of individual products.

Examples

- Warehouse direct costs (eg space costs)
- Transport direct costs (eg fuel)
- Store/supermarket direct costs (eg shelf filling)

Confusingly, direct product costs also contain some level of indirect cost, apportioned on the basis of product characteristics (eg cost of shelf space apportioned by means of physical volume).

| Activity based costing (ABC) | Customer profitability analysis (CPA) | Direct product profitability (DPP) | **Activity based management (ABM)** | Behavioural aspects |

Activity based management (ABM)

The management processes that use the information provided by an activity based cost analysis to improve organisational profitability

The goal of ABM is to enable customer needs to be satisfied while making fewer demands on organisational resources.

How organisational profitability is improved

- Cost reduction
- Cost modelling
- Identification and focus on key processes
- Identification of non-value added activities (which can then be reduced, scrapped or outsourced)

Example

The non-value added activity of a customer complaints service is totally unnecessary and is dependent on inadequate processes.

| Activity based costing (ABC) | Customer profitability analysis (CPA) | Direct product profitability (DPP) | Activity based management (ABM) | **Behavioural aspects** |

Overhead absorption rates can be manipulated and used to influence behaviour.

Example 1
Traditionally, a direct labour cost percentage absorption rate has been used to keep labour costs down.

Example 2
If an organisation's policy is to automate, use of a direct labour hour absorption rate should encourage managers to shed labour in favour of automation.

Example 3
If overheads are absorbed on the basis of the number of component parts a product contains, product designers might be influenced to use fewer components.

Example 4
By splitting annual stock holding costs evenly between the number of components held, there should be a strong incentive for designers to use standard components.

Notes

8: Standard costing

Topic List

- Mix and yield variances
- Planning and operational variances
- ABC and overhead variances
- Learning curve
- Behavioural implications
- Standard costing in the modern environment

Some of the contents of this chapter should be familiar from your Paper 8 studies. Other aspects will be completely new to you. It is vital that you are 100% happy with the basic variances covered in Paper 8, however, before you can fully understand the variances covered in Paper 9.

> Key questions to try in the kit: 43, 45, 46
> Refer to MCQ cards (with Chs 7 & 9):
> 66 - 109

| Mix and yield variances | Planning and operational variances | ABC and overhead variances | Learning curve | Behavioural implications | Standard costing in the modern environment |

If a product requires two or more raw materials, and the proportions of the materials are changeable and controllable, the materials usage variance can be split into a mix of a mix variance and a yield variance.

Materials yield variance

- A measure of the effect on costs of inputs yielding more or less than expected
- Calculated as the difference between the expected output and the actual output, valued at the standard cost per unit of output

Calculating the yield variance

1. Find, for one unit of output, the standard *total* materials usage in kgs, litres etc, and the cost of this standard usage.
2. Determine the standard output from the actual total quantity input.

Example

1 Std input to produce 1 unit of X:

A	20 kgs × £10	£200
B	30 kgs × £5	£150
	50 kgs	£350

In May, 13 units of X were produced from 250kg of A and 350 kgs of B.

2 (250+350)kgs should have

yielded (÷ 50kgs)	12X
but did yield	13X
Yield variance in units	1X (F)
× standard cost per unit of output	× £350
Yield variance in £	£350 (F)

Materials mix variance

- A measure of whether the actual mix is cheaper or more expensive than the standard
- Calculated as the difference between the actual total quantity used in the standard mix and the actual quantity used in the actual mix, **valued** using one of two methods

  EITHER   **Standard input price of each material**

  OR   **The difference between the standard weighted average price and the individual standard input prices**

Calculating the mix variance

1. Find the standard proportions of the mix.
2. Calculate the standard mix of the actual materials used.
3. Find (in kgs, litres etc for each input, the differences between what should have been used and what was used.
4. Value the variances using one of the two methods.

These two approaches are recommended by CIMA (CIMA *Insider*, October 2001). Either or both valuation methods may be tested: the requirements of the question will specify the required approach. For example a question in the November 2001 (Paper 8) exam specified the weighted average valuation method.

| Mix and yield variances | Planning and operational variances | ABC and overhead variances | Learning curve | Behavioural implications | Standard costing in the modern environment |

Example (cont'd from page 80)

	Material A	Material B
Mix should have been (600 kgs split 2:3)	240 kgs	360 kgs
But was	250 kgs	350 kgs
Mix variance in kgs	10 kgs (A)	10 kgs (F)

Valuation at standard input prices

	Material A	Material B
Mix variance in kgs	10 kgs (A)	10 kgs (F)
× std cost per kg (say)	× £10	× £5
	£100 (A)	£50 (F)

Valuation at difference between standard weighted average price and individual standard input prices

Using information from Step 1 in the example on page 80, the standard weighted average price = £350/50 = £7.

	Material A	Material B
Mix variance in kgs	10 kgs (A)	10 kgs (F)
× difference in prices	× £(7 – 10)	× £(7 – 5)
	£30 (A)	£20 (A)

The total mix variance in quantity (here 10 kgs (A) + 10 kgs (F)) is always zero.

The total mix variance (in £) is the same by both methods, but the individual mix variances are different.

The overall mix variance (in £) is adverse because more of the more expensive material was used than anticipated.

Actual usage compared with standard	Standard input price compared with weighted average price	Variance
More (A)	Greater	(A)
More (A)	Less	(F)
Less (F)	Greater	(F)
Less (F)	Less	(A)

Remember you must be able to use both methods of valuation.

| Mix and yield variances | Planning and operational variances | ABC and overhead variances | Learning curve | Behavioural implications | Standard costing in the modern environment |

Labour mix variance

- Also known as the **team composition variance**
- A measure of whether the actual mix of labour grades is cheaper or more expensive than the standard mix
- Calculated in exactly the same way as the materials mix variance

> As with the materials mix variance, CIMA requires you to be able to value the labour mix variance in two ways.

Labour yield variance

- Also known as the **team productivity variance**
- Shows how productively people are working
- Calculated in exactly the same way as the materials yield variance

Example

Standard hours for actual mix: 85 hours of grade A labour
Actual hours: 90 hours of grade A labour
Weighted average rate per hour: £15
Standard rate per hour for grade A labour: £13

Using the weighted average method, the mix variance for grade A labour is favourable because more hours than standard were worked at a standard rate less than the weighted average rate.

Using the standard input rate method, however, the mix variance for grade A labour would be adverse because more hours than standard were worked.

| Mix and yield variances | **Planning and operational variances** | ABC and overhead variances | Learning curve | Behavioural implications | Standard costing in the modern environment |

Planning variances

- Arise because of inaccurate planning/faulty standards and so not controllable by operational managers but by senior management
- Calculated by comparing an original standard with a revised standard

Disadvantages

- ☒ Difficulty in determining realistic standards
- ☒ Danger of managers attempting to explain all variances as planning errors
- ☒ Time-consuming preparation
- ☒ Do not provide an overall picture of the total variance

Advantages

- ☑ Highlight controllable and uncontrollable variances
- ☑ Increase both managers' acceptance of the use of variances for performance measurement and managers' motivation
- ☑ Improve planning and standard-setting processes as standards are more accurate, relevant and appropriate
- ☑ Operational variances provide a fairer reflection of actual performance

Operational variances

- Caused by adverse/favourable operational performance
- Calculated by comparing actual results with a realistic, revised standard/budget

| Mix and yield variances | **Planning and operational variances** | ABC and overhead variances | Learning curve | Behavioural implications | Standard costing in the modern environment |

Total planning and operational variances

Example

The standard material cost of a product is £3 (3 kgs × £1). Actual material costs were £250,000 when 70,000 units were made and 200,000 kgs of material were used. With the benefit of hindsight, management realise that a more realistic standard material cost for current conditions would be £4.20 (3.5 kgs × £1.20).

	£
Revised standard cost (70,000 × £4.20)	294,000
Original standard cost (70,000 × £3)	210,000
Total planning variance	**84,000 (A)**

These total variances can both be split into sub-variances.

	£
70,000 units should have cost (using revised std of £4.20)	294,000
but did cost	250,000
Total operational variance	**44,000 (F)**

Planning sub-variances

There are two ways to value the two planning sub-variances.

Example cont'd

Planning price variance

= (orig std price − rev std price) × rev std usage
= (£1.00 − £1.20) × 245,000kg
= £49,000 (A)

Planning usage variance

= (orig std usage − rev std usage) × orig std price
= (70,000 × (3kgs − 3.5 kgs)) × £1
= £35,000 (A)

Total planning variance =
£84,000 (A)

Example cont'd

Planning price variance

= (orig std price − rev std price) × orig std usage
= (£1.00 − £1.20) × (70,000 × 3kgs)
= £42,000 (A)

Planning usage variance

= (orig std usage − revised std usage) × rev std price
= (70,000 × (3 kgs − 3.5kgs)) × £1.20
= £42,000 (A)

Total planning variance =
£84,000 (A)

Operational sub-variances

Example cont'd

	£
200,000 kgs should have cost (× £1.20 revised std)	240,000
but did cost	250,000
Material price variance	10,000 (A)

70,000 units should have used (× 3.5 kgs revised std)	245,000 kg
but did use	200,000 kg
Variance in kgs	45,000 kg (F)
× std cost per kg (rev std)×	£1.20
Material usage variance	£54,000 (F)

| Mix and yield variances | **Planning and operational variances** | ABC and overhead variances | Learning curve | Behavioural implications | Standard costing in the modern environment |

Sales volume and selling price variances

- **Planning** – compare original budgeted and revised budgeted sales volumes/revenue
- **Operational** – compare revised budgeted and actual sales volumes/revenue

> The format of a management report which includes planning and operational variances should be tailored to the information needs of the managers who receive it. Senior management need to review performance as a whole. A layout which identifies all planning variances together and then all operational variances may be most illuminating.
>
> - The difference due to planning is the responsibility of planners
> - The remainder of difference is the responsibility of functional managers

Management reports

X LTD OPERATING STATEMENT

	£	£
Original budget contribution		X
Planning variances		
Material usage etc		X
Revised budget contribution		X
Sales volume variance		X
Revised std cont'n from sales achieved		X
Operational variances		
Labour efficiency etc		X
Actual contribution		X
Fixed costs budget	X	
Expenditure variance	X	
		X
Actual margin		X

| Mix and yield variances | Planning and operational variances | **ABC and overhead variances** | Learning curve | Behavioural implications | Standard costing in the modern environment |

All overheads within an ABC system are treated as variable.

If the overhead varies with production volume, the calculation of variances in the same as the traditional approach for variable overheads.

If the **overhead varies with some other activity**:

- **Expenditure variances** are the difference between what the expenditure should have been for the actual level of activity (actual level of activity x cost driver rate) and the actual expenditure.
- **Efficiency variances** are the difference between the level of activity that should have been needed and the actual activity level, valued at the standard rate per activity (ie at the cost driver rate).

| Mix and yield variances | Planning and operational variances | ABC and overhead variances | **Learning curve** | Behavioural implications | Standard costing in the modern environment |

Theory

As **cumulative output doubles**, the **cumulative average time per unit** produced **falls** to a fixed percentage of the previous cumulative average time per unit.

When does learning curve theory apply?

- Product made largely by labour effort
- Brand new or relativity short-lived product
- Complex product made in small quantities for special orders

> Note that cumulative average time = average time per unit for all units produce so far, back to and including the first unit made.

Example

Assume a 90% learning effect applies.

Cumulative output Units		Cumulative average time per unit Hours		Total time required Hours	Incremental time taken Total hours		Hours/unit
1		50.00	(× 1)	50.0			
2*	(× 90%)	45.00	(× 2)	90.0	40.0	(÷ 1)	40.0
4*	(× 90%)	40.50	(× 4)	162.0	72.0	(÷ 2)	36.0
8*	(× 90%)	36.45	(× 8)	291.6	129.6	(÷ 4)	32.4

* Output doubled each time

Graph of the learning effect

The learning effect can be shown as a learning curve, either for unit times (graph (a)) or for cumulative times or costs (graph (b)).

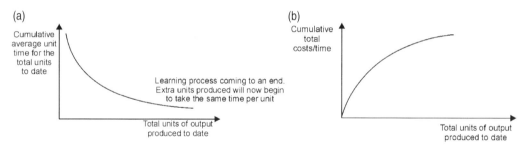

Curve (a) becomes horizontal once a sufficient number of units have been produced (ie the learning effect is lost). Production time should become a constant standard, to which a standard efficiency rate may be applied.

| Mix and yield variances | Planning and operational variances | ABC and overhead variances | **Learning curve** | Behavioural implications | Standard costing in the modern environment |

Formula for the learning curve

The formula for learning curve (a) shown above is
$Y_x = aX^b$

where Y = cumulative average time per unit

X = the number of units made so far

a = the time for the first unit

b = the learning coefficient or index
   = log of learning rate / log of 2

This formula will be provided in the exam if it is needed.

Costs affected by the learning curve effect

- As the learning effect is a function of labour, only labour costs and other variable costs directly dependent on labour are affected.
- Materials should not be affected unless early on in the learning process they are used inefficiently.
- Fixed overhead expenditure should be unaffected (but some problems might be caused in an organisation that uses absorption costing).

Where the learning effect might impact

- Sales projections, advertising expenditure and delivery date commitments
- Recruitment of new labour
- Calculation of productivity bonus
- Work scheduling and overtime decisions
- Budgeting with standard costs
- Cash flow projections (reducing unit variable costs)
- Market share

Where learning curve theory can be used

- To calculate the marginal (incremental) cost of making extra units of a product
- To quote selling prices for a contract, where prices are calculated at a cost plus a percentage mark-up for profit
- To prepare realistic production budgets and more efficient production schedules
- To prepare realistic standard costs for cost control purposes

| Mix and yield variances | Planning and operational variances | ABC and overhead variances | **Learning curve** | Behavioural implications | Standard costing in the modern environment |

Cost experience curves

> The term applied to the 'corporate embodiment' of the shop floor, managerial and technological learning effects within an organisation.

It expresses the way in which the average cost per unit of production changes over time due to technological and organisational changes, not just 'learning' by skilled workers.

- Material costs will decrease slightly due to quantity discounts.
- Variable overheads will follow the pattern of direct labour.
- As volumes increase, fixed overhead per unit falls.

It is best exploited by growth and achieving a sizeable market share, so that an organisation can benefit from mass production techniques.

Limitations of learning curve theory

- Learning curve effect is not always present.
- It assumes stable conditions which allow learning to take place.
- It assumes a certain degree of motivation amongst employees.
- Breaks between repeating production of an item must not be too long or workers will forget and learning will have to begin again.
- It may be difficult to obtain enough accurate data to decide what the learning factor is.
- Learning will eventually cease.

| Mix and yield variances | Planning and operational variances | ABC and overhead variances | Learning curve | **Behavioural implications** | Standard costing in the modern environment |

Features of good feedback

- Clear, comprehensive, timely and accurate
- Exception principle
- Highlights controllable costs/revenues
- 'Bad news' carefully relayed and discussed
- Specific rather than general
- Credible source

Problems related to the interdependencies between variances can be addressed by ensuring managers are aware of the wider implications of their actions, or by placing less emphasis on the 'control' and 'responsibility' aspects of variances and more on their role as aid to management.

Reasons for poor attitudes to control information

- Seen as low priority
- Resentment (system of trying to find fault)
- Seen as pressure device
- False sense of objectives
- Flaws in recording of actual costs
- Received too late

Ways of using budgetary information to evaluate performance

- Budget constrained
- Profit conscious
- Non-accounting

| Mix and yield variances | Planning and operational variances | ABC and overhead variances | Learning curve | Behavioural implications | **Standard costing in the modern environment** |

Question 1: How appropriate is the use of standard costing in today's business environment?

Standard costing	Modern environment
Most appropriate in a stable, standardised repetitive environment with homogenous output	More sophisticated customer requirements and increased competition require rapid rate of change in product type/design, with short product life cycles
Focus on quantity	Focus on quality

Question 2: Can standard costing and TQM coexist?

Standard costing	Modern environment
Predetermined standards	Continual improvement
Stable, standardised repetitive environment	Improvements to input quantities etc
Planned level of scrap	Zero defects
Attainable standards	Elimination of waste

Question 3: How can standard costing be used today?

- Planning
- Control
- Decision making
- Performance measurement
- Product pricing
- Improvement and change
- Accounting valuations

9: Costing systems for modern manufacturing

Topic List

Costing systems and manufacturing

Theory of constraints (TOC)

Throughput accounting (TA)

Life cycle costing

Backflush costing

Target costing

The techniques covered in this chapter and the previous one are relatively new and may appear to solve a lot of the problems faced by management today. It is up to you to decide whether you think they are radical new ideas or just a case of the 'emperor's new clothes'!

> Key questions to try in the kit:
> 51, 52, 56, 59
> Refer to MCQ cards (with Chs 7 & 8):
> 66 - 109

| Costing systems and manufacturing | Theory of constraints (TOC) | Throughput accounting (TA) | Life cycle costing | Backflush costing | Target costing |

Costing systems

- Costing systems are designed to compliment the organisation's operations flow.

- They provide management information for planning and control on a daily, monthly or long-term basis.

- Changes in manufacturing philosophy and new technology (CAM and FMS) require changes in information and cost reporting systems.

  - Collecting information in a different way
  - Rethinking what data needs to be collected
  - Rethinking what data needs to be reported

New systems

- Unit quantities (rather than monthly £ values) are reported to production employees.

- Performance measures based on output (rather than hours worked) are reported to management.

Manufacturing philosophy

Traditional versus Modern

Traditional

- Labour and equipment are so valuable they should not be left idle.
- Resulting stock not needed should be stored (hiding inefficient and uneven production).
- Large batch sizes/production runs increase efficiency and reduce cost per unit.
- Production run costs and stock holding costs need to be balanced.

Modern

- Smooth, steady production flow (throughput)
- Flexibility (to meet customer demands), with the result that the organisation is more complex
- Volume versus variety (see Chapter 7)
- JIT (covered in detail in Paper 8)

| Costing systems and manufacturing | **Theory of constraints (TOC)** | Throughput accounting (TA) | Life cycle costing | Backflush costing | Target costing |

Theory of constraints (TOC)

An **approach to production management** which aims to maximise sales revenue less material and variable overhead costs. It focuses on the factors which act as constraints to this maximisation.

Binding constraint

A process that acts as a bottleneck (or limiting factor) and constrains throughput

Principles

Stock costs money in terms of storage space and interest and so is undesirable.

- The only stock that should be held is a buffer stock immediately prior to the bottleneck so that output through it is never held up.
- Operations prior to the binding constraint should operate at the same speed as the binding constraint otherwise WIP will build up.

Aim

Maximise **throughput contribution** (sales revenue less material cost) while keeping **conversion cost** (all operating costs accept material cost) and **investment cost** (stock, equipment, building costs etc) to a minimum.

TOC is not an accounting system. It is a production system.

| Costing systems and manufacturing | Theory of constraints (TOC) | **Throughput accounting (TA)** | Life cycle costing | Backflush costing | Target costing |

Throughput accounting (TA)

An **approach to accounting**, in line with the JIT philosophy, which assumes management have a given set of resources available (existing buildings, capital equipment, labour force). Using these resources, purchased materials and parts must be processed to generate sales revenue. The most appropriate financial objective to set is therefore maximisation of throughput (sales revenue less direct material cost).

Why is TA different?

TA differs from other accounting systems because of what it **emphasises**.

- 1st Throughput
- 2nd Stock minimisation
- 3rd Cost control

Examples

Throughput accounting can be used successfully in service and retail industries.

- If there is a delay in processing a potential customer's application, business can be lost.
- A bottleneck might form if work that could be done by nurses has to be carried out by doctors.

| Costing systems and manufacturing | Theory of constraints (TOC) | **Throughput accounting (TA)** | Life cycle costing | Backflush costing | Target costing |

Three concepts upon which TA is based

1. All factory costs except materials costs are fixed.

2. The ideal inventory level is zero (apart from a buffer stock prior to the bottleneck) and so unavoidable idle capacity is inevitable.

3. No value is added and no profit is made until a sale takes place.

Factors that limit throughput

- Bottleneck resources
- Lack of product quality/reliability
- Unreliable material supplies
- Customers with particular demands

Throughput measures

- **Return per time period***

  Throughput contribution ÷ time period

- **Return per time period on bottleneck resource***

  Throughput contribution ÷ minutes (say) on bottleneck resource

- **TA ratio***

  Throughput contribution per time period ÷ conversion cost (ie labour + o/head) per time period

- **Current effectiveness ratio**

  Standard minutes of throughput achieved ÷ minutes available

* Based on **throughput contribution** or **return** or **value added** = sales − material costs

Criticisms

- It is seen by some as too short term, as all costs other than direct material cost are regarded as fixed.
- It concentrates on direct material cost and does not control other costs.
- By attempting to maximise throughput an organisation could be producing in excess of profit-maximising output.

Advantages

The principal advantage of TA is that it directs attention to critical factors.

- Bottlenecks
- Key elements in making profit
- Inventory reduction
- Reducing response time to customer demand
- Even production flow
- Overall effectiveness and efficiency

| Costing systems and manufacturing | Theory of constraints (TOC) | Throughput accounting (TA) | **Life cycle costing** | Backflush costing | Target costing |

The product life cycle

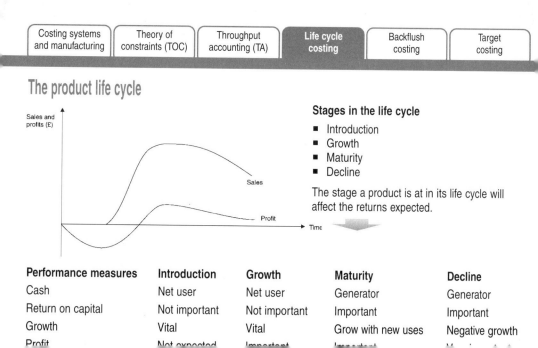

Stages in the life cycle
- Introduction
- Growth
- Maturity
- Decline

The stage a product is at in its life cycle will affect the returns expected.

Performance measures	Introduction	Growth	Maturity	Decline
Cash	Net user	Net user	Generator	Generator
Return on capital	Not important	Not important	Important	Important
Growth	Vital	Vital	Grow with new uses	Negative growth
Profit	Not expected	Important	Important	

Life cycle costing

The profiling of cost over a product's life, including the pre-production stage

How to maximise the return over the product life cycle

- Design costs out of products
- Minimise the time to market
- Minimise breakeven time
- Maximise the length of the life span
- Minimise product proliferation

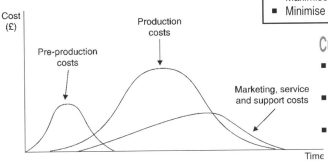

Customer life cycle

- Aim is to extend the life cycle of a particular customer.
- Do this by encouraging loyalty (eg loyalty cards).
- Customers become more profitable over their life cycle (eg bank customers).

| Costing systems and manufacturing | Theory of constraints (TOC) | Throughput accounting (TA) | **Life cycle costing** | Backflush costing | Target costing |

Traditional management accounting systems v Life cycle costing

- Traditional management accounting systems are based on the financial year and so dissect the product life cycle into a series of annual sections. This means that profitability is assessed on an annual basis.
- Such systems total all non-production costs and record them as a period expense.
- They write off R&D expenditure against revenue from existing products so that existing products seem less profitable and are scrapped too quickly.

- This approach tracks and accumulates a product's actual costs and revenues over the entire product life cycle, which means that a product's total profitability can be determined.
- It traces non-production costs to individual products over complete life cycles.

Benefits of life cycle costing

- Full understanding of individual product profitability
- More accurate feedback information
- Cost reduction/minimisation and revenue expansion opportunities more apparent
- Increased visibility of non-production costs

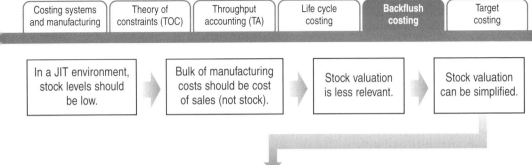

So far there have been MCQs on this topic, rather than long questions.

| Costing systems and manufacturing | Theory of constraints (TOC) | Throughput accounting (TA) | Life cycle costing | **Backflush costing** | Target costing |

Accounting entries

- One or two **trigger points** determine when entries are made in the accounting system.
  - When materials are purchased/received (but not in a true JIT system where no stocks are held)
  - When goods are completed/sold
- Actual conversion costs are recorded as incurred.
- Conversion costs are applied to products at the second trigger point based on standard cost.
- Any conversion costs not applied to products are c/f and disposed of at the period end.
- The WIP account is eliminated.

> The successful operation of backflush costing rests upon predictable levels of efficiency and stable material prices and usage (ie no significant cost variances).

Problems with backflush costing

- ☒ It is only acceptable for external financial reporting if stocks are low or practically unchanged from one period to the next.
- ☒ Production controls are needed to ensure cost control during the production process.
- ☒ It is only appropriate if production and sales are approximately equal.

Advantages of backflush costing

- ☑ It is simple.
- ☑ The number of accounting entries is greatly reduced.
- ☑ It should discourage managers from producing simply for stock.

Example: two trigger points

				£	£
Purchase of raw materials	£16,000	DR	Raw materials control	16,000	
Conversion costs incurred	£12,700	CR	Creditors		16,000
Sales and production	5,000 units				
		DR	Conversion costs control	12,700	
No opening stock of raw materials, WIP or finished goods		CR	Creditors		12,700
	£	DR	Finished goods stock (5,000 × £5.80)	29,000	
Standard cost per unit		CR	Raw materials control (5,000 × £3.20)		16,000
Raw materials	3.20	CR	Conversion costs allocated (5,000 × £2.60)		13,000
Conversion costs	2.60	DR	Cost of goods sold (5,000 × £5.80)	29,000	
	5.80	CR	Finished goods stock		29,000
		DR	Conversion costs allocated	13,000	
		CR	Cost of goods sold		300
		CR	Conversion costs control		12,700

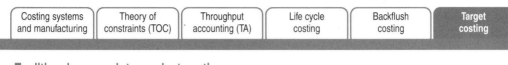

Traditional approach to product costing

1. Develop a product
2. Determine the expected standard production cost
3. Set a selling price (probably based on cost)
4. Resulting profit

Costs are controlled through variance analysis at monthly intervals.

versus

Target costing approach

Competitive market price — Set according to what the competition is charging or, if the product is new, set using market research or **functional analysis/pricing by function**

− Desired profit margin — As determined by the organisation's short-, medium- and long-term plans

= **Target cost** — Resulting cost that must be achieved

Target cost

When a product is first manufactured, the target cost may be well below currently achievable cost but management will set benchmarks for improvement towards the target cost by specified dates and will incorporate them into the budgeting process.

Options available to reduce cost

- Develop the product in an atmosphere of continuous improvement.
- Apply value engineering techniques.
- Collaborate closely with suppliers.
- Change production methods.
- Improve technologies/processes.
- Cut out non-value added activities.

Even if the product can be produced to target cost, once it goes into production the target cost will gradually be reduced. The reductions will be incorporated into the budgeting process, which means that cost savings must be actively sought. **Value analysis** can be used to reduce costs if and when targets are missed.

Notes

10: Investment appraisal: basic principles

Topic List

Capital budgeting process

Post-completion audit/appraisal

Payback and ARR methods

Net present value (NPV) method

Internal rate of return (IRR) method

DCF: additional points

Capital expenditure differs from day to day revenue expenditure because it often involves a bigger outlay and the benefits from it are likely to accrue over a long period of time. Any proposed capital expenditure should therefore be properly appraised and found to be worthwhile before the decision is taken to go ahead with the expenditure.

> Key questions to try in the kit: 62, 66
> Refer to MCQ cards (with Chs 11 & 12):
> 110 - 150

| **Capital budgeting process** | Post-completion audit/appraisal | Payback and ARR methods | Net present value (NPV) method | Internal rate of return (IRR) method | DCF: additional points |

Capital budgeting process

> This topic has yet to be examined in depth.

1 Evaluate the project

- Initial screening
  - 'Fit' with organisation's long-term objectives
  - Resources required and their availability
  - Risk
  - Alternatives
  - Purpose
  - Time frame
  - Availability of suitable management expertise
  - Key factors to success
- Detailed financial analysis (involving application of appraisal techniques)

2 Consider any qualitative factors

- Effect on company's image
- Implications of not undertaking the investment

3 Approve project

- Suitably qualified manager to have responsibility for project progress
- Senior management to give backing

4 Monitor and control the progress of approved projects

- Control over excess spending
  - The authority to make capital expenditure decisions should be formally assigned.
  - Capital expenditure decisions should be documented and properly approved
  - If actual expenditure exceeds the amount authorised by a permitted percentage, re-authorisation should be required.
  - Authorisation of any capital expenditure which would take total spending above the total capital budget should be referred to board level, for example, for approval.

- Control over delays
  - If capital expenditure has not taken place before a stated deadline is reached, the project should be resubmitted for fresh authorisation.
  - The proposer should be asked to explain reasons for the delay.

- Control over anticipated benefits
  - Ensure anticipated benefits do actually materialise, benefits are as big as anticipated and running costs do not exceed expectation.
  - The difficulty in controlling projects, however, is that they are usually 'unique', with no standard or yardstick against which to judge them.

| Capital budgeting process | **Post-completion audit/appraisal** | Payback and ARR methods | Net present value (NPV) method | Internal rate of return (IRR) method | DCF: additional points |

Post-completion audit/appraisal

> 'An objective and independent appraisal of the measure of success of a capital expenditure project in progressing the business as planned. The appraisal should cover the implementation of the project from authorisation to commissioning and its technical and commercial performance after commissioning. The information provided is also used by management as feedback which aids the implementation and control of future projects.'
> *(Official Terminology)*

Question 1: Why?

- The threat of post audit will motivate managers to work to achieve the project benefits promised.
- If carried out before the end of the project life it can improve efficiency/increase benefits or highlight those projects which should be discontinued.
- It can help to identify those managers who have been good/bad performers.
- Weaknesses in forecasting/estimating techniques may be identified.

Question 2: Which?

- Managers should perceive that every project has the chance of being audited.
- A reasonable guideline might be to audit all projects above a certain size and a random selection of smaller projects.
- A post audit should concentrate on those aspects of an investment which have been identified as particularly sensitive/critical to the success of the project.
- Consider cost/benefit trade-off.

Question 3: When?

An audit should not be carried out too soon (information is incomplete) or too late (management action is delayed and the usefulness of information reduced).

Problems

- Impact of uncontrollable factors
- Difficulty in separating costs and benefits
- Costly and time consuming
- If applied punitively, managers may become over cautious/risk averse
- Difficulty in identifying long-term strategic effects of projects

Alternative control processes

- Teams could manage a project from beginning to end.
- More time could be spent choosing projects.

| Capital budgeting process | Post-completion audit/appraisal | **Payback and APR methods** | Net present value (NPV) method | Internal rate of return (IRR) method | DCF: additional points |

Payback

> The time it takes the cash inflows (≈ profits before depreciation) for an investment to equal the cash outflows, usually expressed in years

It is often used as a first screening method, the project being evaluated with a more sophisticated technique if it gets through the payback test.

Decision rules

1. **When deciding between two or more competing projects, the usual decision is to accept the one with the shortest payback.**
2. **Reject a project if its payback is greater than a target payback.**

Disadvantages

- ☒ It ignores the timing of cash flows within the payback period, the cash flows after the end of the payback period and hence the total project return.
- ☒ It ignores the time value of money.
- ☒ It makes no distinction between different projects with the same payback period.
- ☒ The choice of cut-off payback period is arbitrary.
- ☒ The method may lead to excessive investment in short-term projects.
- ☒ It takes account of the risk associated with the timing of cash flows but not the variability of those cash flows.

Advantages

- ☑ Long payback means capital is tied up.
- ☑ A focus on early payback can enhance liquidity.
- ☑ Investment risk is increased if payback is longer.
- ☑ Shorter-term forecasts are likely to be more reliable.
- ☑ The calculation is quick and simple.
- ☑ Payback is an easily understood concept.

| Capital budgeting process | Post-completion audit/appraisal | **Payback and APR methods** | Net present value (NPV) method | Internal rate of return (IRR) method | DCF: additional points |

Accounting rate of return (ARR)

There are several definitions of ARR (the method selected should be used consistently) but the recommended definition is

$$ARR = \frac{\text{Average annual profits from an investment}}{\text{Average investment}} \times 100\%$$

- Annual profits are after depreciation
- Average investment = ½(initial cost − residual value)

If you are not provided with a figure for profit, assume that net cash inflow minus depreciation equals profit.

Decision rules

- *One* project
  - If the ARR is greater than the target rate of return, accept the project.
  - If the ARR is less than the target rate of return, reject the project.

- When comparing *two or more mutually exclusive projects*, the project with the highest ARR should be chosen (provided the ARR is greater than the target ARR).

Advantages

- ☑ Quick and simple
- ☑ Looks at the entire project life
- ☑ Easily calculated from financial statements

Disadvantages

- ☒ Takes no account of the timing of cash flows
- ☒ Based on accounting profits which are subject to a number of different accounting treatments
- ☒ Takes no account of the size of the investment or the length of the project
- ☒ Ignores the time value of money

Example

Equipment J has a capital cost of £100,000 and a disposal value of £20,000 at the end of its five-year life. Profits before depreciation over the five years total £150,000.

∴ Total profit after depreciation = £(150,000 − 80,000) = £70,000

Average annual profit after depreciation = £14,000

(Capital cost + disposal cost) / 2 = £60,000

ARR = (14/70) × 100% = 20%

| Capital budgeting process | Post-completion audit/appraisal | Payback and ARR methods | **Net present value (NPV) method** | Internal rate of return (IRR) method | DCF: additional points |

Present value

The cash equivalent now (X) of a sum of money (V) receivable or payable at the end of n time periods

Discounting provides the formula $X = V/(1+r)^n$, where r is the rate of return.

Net present value

The value obtained by discounting all cash inflows and outflows of a capital investment project by a chosen target rate of return

The NPV is based on cash flows of a project, not accounting profits.

Decision rules

- *One* project
  - If NPV > 0 ➡ accept project
  - If NPV < 0 ➡ reject project
- When comparing *two or more mutually exclusive projects*, the project with the highest positive NPV should be selected.

Assumptions in the NPV model

- Forecasts are certain.
- Information is freely available and costless.
- The discount rate is a measure of the opportunity cost of funds which ensures wealth maximisation for *all* individuals and companies.

Discount factors

Present value tables cover integer costs of capital from 1% to 20% for 1 to 20 years. If you require a discount factor for a non-integer interest rate (say 12.5%) or a period of time greater than 20 years, use $1/(1+r)^n$, where r = cost of capital and n = number of years.

Timing of cash flows

- A cash outlay to be incurred at the beginning of an investment project ('**now**') occurs at time 0 and will have a present value = outlay (since PV of £1 now = £1).
- A cash flow occurring **during the course of a time period** is assumed to occur at the end of the time period.
- A cash flow occurring **at the beginning of a time period** is assumed to occur at the end of the previous time period.

| Capital budgeting process | Post-completion audit/appraisal | Payback and ARR methods | **Net present value (NPV) method** | Internal rate of return (IRR) method | DCF: additional points |

Perpetuities

> An annual cash flow in perpetuity

The PV of £1 pa in perpetuity at r% = £1/r (where r is a decimal).

Net terminal value (NTV)

> The cash surplus remaining at the end of a project after taking account of interest and capital repayments

The NTV discounted at the cost of capital = NPV

Annuities

> A constant annual cash flow from year to year

Use discount factors from **cumulative present value tables**.

Example

PV of £1,000 in years 2 to 6 at a rate of r% =

$$£1,000 \times \begin{cases} \text{PV of £1 pa for yrs 1–6 at r\%} = & X \\ \text{PV of £1 pa for yrs 1–2 at r\%} = & (X) \\ \text{PV of £1 pa for yrs 2–6 at r\%} = & \underline{\underline{X}} \end{cases}$$

| Capital budgeting process | Post-completion audit/appraisal | Payback and ARR methods | Net present value (NPV) method | **Internal rate of return (IRR) method** | DCF: additional points |

IRR (or DCF yield)

> The rate of interest at which the NPV of an investment is zero

Decision rule

If the IRR is greater than the target rate of return, the project is worth undertaking.

IRR of a perpetuity

- IRR = perpetuity ÷ initial investment

IRR of an annuity

- Cumulative PV factor for years 1 to n at rate r = initial investment ÷ annuity = X
- Look in cumulative PV tables along line for year n to find discount factor corresponding to X
- Corresponding rate = IRR

Example

An investment now of £300,000 will produce inflows of £80,000 per annum over the next five years. To find the IRR:

£300,000 = PV of £80,000 for years 1-5 at rate r

∴ £300,000 = (cumulative PV factor for years 1-5 at rate r) × £80,000

∴ 3.75 = cumulative PV factor for years 1 to 5 at rate r

Find 3.75 in the row for year 5. The corresponding rate is the IRR.

| Capital budgeting process | Post-completion audit/appraisal | Payback and ARR methods | Net present value (NPV) method | **Internal rate of return (IRR) method** | DCF: additional points |

Interpolation method

1. Calculate the NPV using a rough indicator of the IRR ($^2/_3$ (or $^3/_4$) × ARR).

   — Remember you will need to account for depreciation and any residual value when determining the ARR.

2. If the resulting NPV > 0, recalculate the NPV using a higher rate.

3. If the resulting NPV < 0, recalculate the NPV using a lower rate.

   — The closer these NPVs are to zero, the closer the estimate to the true IRR.

4. $$IRR = A + \left[\frac{P}{P+N} \times (B-A)\right]\%$$

   where A = (lower) rate of return with positive NPV
   B = (higher) rate of return with negative NPV
   P = amount of positive NPV
   N = absolute value of negative NPV

   — If P = £1,000 and N = −£2,000, P + N = £(1,000 + 2,000) = £3,000

Graphical approach

Suppose a project has the following NPVs at the following discount rates.

Discount rate	NPV
%	£
5	5,300
10	2,900
15	(1,700)
20	(3,200)

These can be easily plotted on a graph.

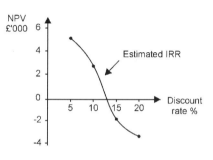

Recalculate the NPV using the estimated IRR (from the graph) of 13% and if the resulting NPV is not equal to, or very near, zero, additional NPVs at different discount rates should be calculated, the graph redrawn and a more accurate IRR determined.

| Capital budgeting process | Post-completion audit/appraisal | Payback and ARR methods | Net present value (NPV) method | Internal rate of return (IRR) method | **DCF: additional points** |

NPV versus IRR

	Which is better?	
	NPV	**IRR**
■ When cash flow patterns are conventional both methods give the same accept or reject decision.	☑	☑
■ The IRR method is more easily understood.		☑
■ IRR and ROCE/ROI can be confused.	☑	
■ IRR ignores the relative sizes of investments.	☑	
■ When cash flow patterns are non-conventional there may be several IRRs of which decision makers must be aware to avoid making the wrong decision.	☑	
■ The NPV method is superior for ranking mutually exclusive projects in order of attractiveness.	☑	
■ When discount rates are expected to differ over the life of the project, such variations can be incorporated easily into NPV calculations but not into IRR calculations.	☑	

Despite the advantages of the NPV method over the IRR method, the IRR method is widely used in practice.

Time value of money

Why is £1 now worth more than £1 in the future?

- Uncertainty
- Inflation
- More weight is attached to current pleasures than to those occurring in the future

Discounted payback

This is the time it will take before a project's cumulative NPV turns from being negative to being positive.

Important issues in investing in IT

- Intangibility of costs and benefits
- Hidden outcomes of investing in IT
- Changing nature of IT systems

Costs to include in project appraisal

The cash flows to consider are the **relevant costs** of the project and could include extra taxation, residual value/disposal value of equipment or its disposal cost and changes in working capital.

Finance-related cash flows are normally excluded: they are only relevant if they incur a different rate of interest from the discount rate.

Advantages of DCF method

- The time value of money is taken into account.
- The method uses all cash flows relating to the project.
- It allows for the timings of cash flows.
- There are universally accepted methods of calculating the NPV and IRR.

Notes

11: Further aspects of investment appraisal

Topic List

Unequal lives

Sensitivity analysis

Life cycle costing
& project abandonment

Inflation

Taxation

Capital rationing

For Paper 9, you need to extend your knowledge of project appraisal beyond both that covered at Foundation level and the basics in Chapter 10 to more complex areas. You are far more likely to encounter an MCQ question on taxation or a long question on sensitivity analysis than a question requiring you to carry out a simple DCF appraisal.

▶ Key questions to try in the kit:
68, 74, 76, 79
Refer to MCQ cards (with Chs 10 & 12):
110 - 150 ◀

| Unequal lives | Sensitivity analysis | Life cycle costing & project abandonment | Inflation | Taxation | Capital rationing |

Annualised equivalents

Enable a comparison to be made between NPVs of projects with different durations

$$= \frac{\text{NPV at r\%}}{\text{Cumulative r\% discount factor for life of project}}$$

Decision rule
Choose the project with the higher annualised equivalent.

Replacement theory

Identical replacement (how frequently)

1. Calculate the PV of costs for each replacement cycle over one cycle only.

2. Turn these PVs of costs into **equivalent annual costs**:

   $$\frac{\text{PV of cost over one replacement cycle}}{\text{Cumulative PV factor for number of years in cycle}}$$

3. The **optimum** replacement cycle is the one with the **lowest** equivalent annual cost.

Non-identical replacement (when)

The best time to replace an existing machine will be the option which gives the lowest NPV of cost in perpetuity, for both the existing machine and the machine which eventually replaces it.

1 Calculate optimum replacement cycle for new machine and its equivalent annual cost (as detailed above).

2 PV of cost in perpetuity of new machine from start of year when it is eventually purchased =

$$\frac{\text{equivalent annual cost}}{r} \quad \text{where } r = \text{cost of capital}$$

3 For each replacement option, discount to time 0 the PV of cost in perpetuity of the new machine and the costs associated with the existing machine (such as relevant running costs and resale value which are dependant upon when it is replaced) by the appropriate discount factor.

4 Choose the option with the lowest PV of cost in perpetuity.

| Unequal lives | **Sensitivity analysis** | Life cycle costing & project abandonment | Inflation | Taxation | Capital rationing |

Sensitivity analysis is one method of analysing the risk surrounding a capital expenditure project. It enables an assessment to be made of how responsive the project's NPV is to changes in the variables used to calculate that NPV, which could include estimated selling price, initial cost, cost of capital, length of project, costs and benefits.

Approach 1: Margin of error approach

1 Calculate the project's NPV.

2 Determine the extent to which key variables may change before the investment results in a negative NPV.

Weaknesses
- The method requires that key variables are considered in isolation which is unrealistic since they are often interdependent.
- It does not examine the probability that any particular variation in costs/revenues might occur.

The sensitivity of an NPV computation to changes in a variable that affects the cashflows is:

$$\frac{\text{NPV of project}}{\text{PV of cashflow affected}} \times 100\%$$

Example

Year	Discount factor 8%	PV of plant cost £	PV of running costs £	PV of savings £	PV of net cash flow £
0	1.000	(7,000)			(7,000)
1	0.926		(1,852)	5,556	3,704
2	0.857		(2,143)	5,999	3,856
		(7,000)	(3,995)	11,555	560

Changes in cash flows which would need to occur for the project to break even (NPV = 0) are as follows.

- Plant costs would need to increase by a PV of £560 = 560/7,000 × 100% = 8%
- Running costs would need to increase by a PV of £560 = 560/3,995 × 100% = 14%
- Savings would need to fall by a PV of £560 = 560/11,555 × 100% = 4.8%

Management should review the estimates of benefits to asses whether or not there is a strong possibility of events occurring which would lead to a negative NPV (the PV of benefits only needs to drop by 4.8% before this happens) and, if the decision is taken to accept the investment, they should pay particular attention to controlling the benefits arising from the project.

| Unequal lives | **Sensitivity analysis** | Life cycle costing & project abandonment | Inflation | Taxation | Capital rationing |

Approach 2: Certainty-equivalent approach

- Expected cash flows are converted to riskless equivalent amounts.
- The greater the risk associated with an expected cash flow, the smaller the certainty-equivalent value (for receipts) or the larger the certainty-equivalent value (for payments).
- The disadvantage of this approach is that the amount of adjustment to each cash flow is decided subjectively.

Approach 3: Use of different cost of money rates/shorter time periods

Use a higher cost of money rate for riskier projects or assess riskier projects over a shorter period of time.

Approach 4: Diagrammatic approach

With the key variable on the horizontal axis, plot a graph to show how a project's NPV (on the vertical axis) changes with changes in the key variable or to compare how sensitive the NPVs of two or more projects are to changes in the key variable. Straight lines can be plotted to approximate to curvilinear behaviour.

Approach 5: Introducing probability

Instead of using point estimates or 'most likely' figures, full probability distributions can be drawn up. Two approaches are then possible.

- Calculate EVs and incorporate them into one NPV calculation.
- Calculate a number of NPVs using each of the options provided in the probability distribution and then calculate an EV of the NPVs.

| Unequal lives | Sensitivity analysis | **Life cycle costing & project abandonment** | Inflation | Taxation | Capital rationing |

Life cycle costing

Aims to achieve optimum asset usage at the lowest possible cost

Whereas traditional investment appraisal concentrates on the earning capacity of an asset in terms of the level of investment, life cycle costing aims to optimise the trade-off between acquisition costs, commissioning costs, operating costs, maintenance costs, disposal costs and so on over the economic lives of each asset option.

Once life cycle costing has been used for capital investment appraisal, the aim of life cycle management should then switch to control (monitoring actual life cycle costs and comparing them with expected costs).

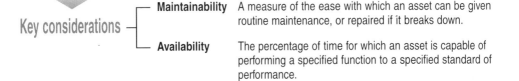

Key considerations

- **Maintainability** — A measure of the ease with which an asset can be given routine maintenance, or repaired if it breaks down.
- **Availability** — The percentage of time for which an asset is capable of performing a specified function to a specified standard of performance.

| Unequal lives | Sensitivity analysis | **Life cycle costing & project abandonment** | Inflation | Taxation | Capital rationing |

Example

Making a decision on the basis of which of two assets has a cheaper purchase price would be a buy-now, pay-later attitude because the cheaper item might cost more to operate and maintain, and might be worth much less on eventual disposal.

Example

A company is choosing between machines X and Y. X costs more but is more reliable than Y. A trade-off must be made between the higher purchase cost and the greater capacity utilisation. (Hospital management might face this sort of decision.)

Project abandonment

A project should be abandoned if it becomes apparent that the present value of the net expected proceeds from abandonment are greater than the present value of the net expected proceeds from continuing the project.

You may need to incorporate the use of decision trees.

Examples of possible complications

- Outcomes in year N determine outcomes in year N + 1, year N + 2 etc
- Buy-back clause
- Events not anticipated at the outset

| Unequal lives | Sensitivity analysis | Life cycle costing & project abandonment | **Inflation** | Taxation | Capital rationing |

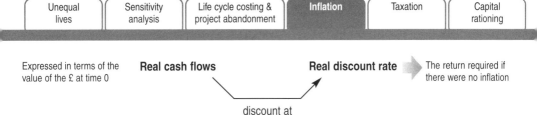

If various costs and benefits do not rise in line with the general level of inflation, apply the money rate to inflated values to determine an NPV.

> **Learn how the two rates are linked!**
> $(1 + \text{money rate}) = (1 + \text{real rate}) \times (1 + \text{inflation rate})$

| Unequal lives | Sensitivity analysis | Life cycle costing & project abandonment | Inflation | **Taxation** | Capital rationing |

Corporation tax

In the UK, under the system being introduced, corporation tax is payable by companies quarterly.

- In the seventh and tenth months of the year in which the profit is earned
- In the first and fourth months of the following year

Half the tax is therefore payable in the year in which the profits are earned and half in the following year.

When taxation is included in DCF calculations, use a post-tax required rate of return.

Example

If a project increases taxable profits by £5,000 in year 4, there will be tax payments of £5,000 × 30% × 50% = £750 in both year 4 and year 5 (assuming a tax rate of 30%).

These tax payments of £750 (a direct result of the project) need to be included in any DCF analysis.

Net cash flows from a project should be considered as the taxable profits arising from a project (unless given an indication to the contrary).

Capital allowances/WDAs

- WDAs reduce taxable profits and hence the tax payable.
- The rate at which WDAs are given will always be provided in the question but it is likely to be 25% on a reducing balance basis.
- The reduction in tax payable (to be included in any DCF analysis) = amount of WDA × tax rate.
- The benefit of WDAs are felt half in the year to which they relate and half in the following year.

> It maybe possible to claim WDAs on the costs of installation as well as original capital costs.

Example

A company purchases a machine costing £80,000. The rate of corporation tax is 30% and WDAs are given on a 25% reducing balance basis.

In year 2, WDA = (£80,000 × 75%) × 25% = £15,000

Tax saved = £15,000 × 30% = £4,500

Benefit received of 50% × £4,500 = £2,250 in both year 2 and year 3

| Unequal lives | Sensitivity analysis | Life cycle costing & project abandonment | Inflation | **Taxation** | Capital rationing |

Balancing allowances/charges

When plant is sold there will be a difference between the sales price and the reducing balance amount at the time of sale.

- Sales price > reducing balance
  ➡ **taxable profit (balancing charge)**
- Sales price < reducing balance
  ➡ **tax allowable loss (balancing allowance)**

Example

A machine has a written down value at the start of year 4 of £15,000. The corporation tax rate is 30%.

- If it is sold for £10,000, there is a balancing allowance of £5,000 which is set against year 4 taxable profits, resulting in a reduction in tax paid of £5,000 × 30% = £1,500, the benefit of which will be received half in year 4 and half in year 5.
- If it is sold for £20,000, the balancing charge of £5,000 will be included in year 4 taxable profits, and tax paid in each of years 4 and 5 will increase by £750.

The balancing allowance/charge should be dealt with in the year of sale.

Taxation and DCF appraisal

1. Calculate **WDAs** and any **balancing allowance/charge.**

2. Based on the WDAs and balancing allowance/charge calculated above, work out the **tax savings** (30% × WDA or allowance) and **tax increase** (30% × charge). These will **affect two years**, the year in which the allowance is claimed or charge occurs and the following year.

3. Calculate the **extra tax** payable **due to savings** related to the project (saving × 30% × 50% in both the year of saving and the following year).

4. Calculate the **tax savings due to non-capital costs** related to the project (cost × 30% × 50% in both the year in which the cost is incurred and the following year).

5. Determine the project's **NPV**, including in the calculation capital cash flows, costs and savings related to the project, taxes on savings and any balancing charge and tax saved on WDAs, any balancing allowances and project costs.

| Unequal lives | Sensitivity analysis | Life cycle costing & project abandonment | Inflation | Taxation | **Capital rationing** |

Capital rationing

If an organisation is in a capital rationing situation, it will not be able to proceed with all projects with positive NPVs because there is not enough capital for all of the investments.

Basic approach

Rank projects in terms of the *profitability index (PI)* =

$$\frac{\text{PV of project's future cash flows}}{\text{PV of total capital outlays}}$$

Key assumptions

- Rationing occurs in a single period.
- Projects cannot be postponed.
- Risk does not impact on project choice.
- Projects are divisible.

Problems with PI method

- It can only be utilised if the projects are divisible.
- The selection takes no account of the strategic value of individual investments in the context of the organisation's objectives.
- It takes no account of cash flow patterns.
- It ignores the absolute size of individual investments.

Example

Project	Investment £'000	PV of inflows £'000	NPV £'000	Ranking per NPV	PI	Ranking per PI
A	100	145	45	2	1.45	2
B	120	168	48	1	1.40	3
C	70	105	35	3	1.50	1

If £200,000 of capital is available, projects C and A should be accepted and $((200 - 170) \div 120) \times 100\%)$ 25% of project B.

Resulting NPV = £1,000(35 + 45 + (25% × 48)) = £92,000

Ranking on the basis of NPV would have resulted in an NPV of £1,000(48 + ($80/100$ × 45)) = £84,000

Always rank on the basis of PI, not NPV.

Notes

12: Investment centre performance appraisal

Topic List

Divisionalisation

Responsibility accounting

Investment centre performance appraisal

Return on investment (ROI) and residual income (RI) are used to appraise both managerial performance within a system of responsibility accounting and divisionalisation with investment centres, and individual projects. Although possibly easier to understand, they are quite seriously flawed when compared with DCF.

Key questions to try in the kit:
82, 85, 89 - 94
Refer to MCQ cards (with Chs 10 & 11):
110 - 150

| Divisionalisation | Responsibility accounting | Investment centre performance appraisal |

There are two common ways of structuring organisations.

- Functionally
- Divisionally

In general, a divisional structure will lead to decentralisation of the decision-making process.

Advantages of divisionalisation

- It can improve the decision-making process in two ways.
  - Quality
  - Speed
- The authority to act to improve performance should motivate divisional managers.
- Top management are freed from detailed involvement in day-to-day operations and can devote more time to strategic planning.
- Divisions provide valuable training grounds for future members of top management.

Disadvantages of divisionalisation

- **Dysfunctional decision making** (a balance has to be kept between decentralisation of authority to provide incentives and motivation, and retaining centralised authority to ensure **goal congruence**)
- Increase in costs of activities common to all divisions
- Loss of control by top management

| | Divisionalisation | **Responsibility accounting** | Investment centre performance appraisal |

Responsibility accounting

> A system of decentralised authority with performance of the decentralised units measured in terms of accounting results

This involves tracing costs (and revenues, assets and liabilities, where appropriate) to the individual managers who are primarily responsible for making decisions about controlling the costs in question.

> The system must therefore distinguish between **controllable costs** and **uncontrollable costs**.

Controllable costs

> Can be influenced by the budget holder

These are three types of responsibility accounting unit/**responsibility centre**.

- Cost centre
- Profit centre
- Investment centre

Increasing decentralisation ↓

	Controllable?
Variable costs	Yes, in the short term
Fixed costs	No (in the short term) or discretionary or directly attributable
Assets/liabilities	To the extent the manager can increase/reduce them

		Investment centre performance appraisal
Divisionalisation	Responsibility accounting	

Return on investment (ROI)

Also known as the **return on capital employed (ROCE)**

> Shows how much profit has been made in relation to the amount of capital invested. It is typically measured as (profit/capital employed) × 100%.

Residual income (RI)

> This is calculated by deducting an imputed interest charge, based on investment in the investment centre, from profit. It is typically measured as follows.
>
> | | £ |
> |---|---|
> | Profit | X |
> | Imputed interest (capital employed × cost of capital) | (X) |
> | Residual income | X |

ROI is generally regarded as the **key performance measure.**

- Ties in directly with the accounting process
- Measures the performance of a division/company as a single entire unit.

Both methods use the same basic figure for profit and investment, but residual income produces an absolute measure whereas the return on investment is expressed as a percentage.

Disadvantages of ROI/RI

1 Both methods suffer from disadvantages in measuring profit and investment.

- The investment can be based on net assets (most usually), gross assets or replacement cost, but none of these bases is ideal.
- Investment centres might use different bases to value stock and to calculate depreciation.
- Any charges made for the use of head office services or allocations of head office assets to investment centres are likely to be arbitrary.

2 These may be problems when bonuses are linked to ROI or RI.

- The measure can be massaged if the asset base of the ratio is altered by increasing/decreasing creditors and debtors (by speeding up/delaying payments and receipts).
- If it is the performance of the manager (rather than the investment centre) being assessed, profit should be based on the revenues/costs controllable by the manager. Service and head office costs should be excluded (except those specifically attributable to the investment centre).

| Divisionalisation | Responsibility accounting | **Investment centre performance appraisal** |

3 The biggest problem in divisional performance measurement occurs if a division maintains the same annual profit, keeps the same assets without a policy of regular fixed asset replacement and values assets at net book value.

ROI or RI will increase year by year as the assets get older, even though profits may be static.

- This can give a false impression of improving performance over time
- It acts to discourage managers from undertaking new investments

Problems with RI in particular

- It does not facilitate comparisons between investment centres.
- It does not relate the size of a centre's income to the size of the investment.

In these respects ROI is a better measure.

Problems with ROI in particular

Problem	How RI can help
Rigid adherence to the need to maintain ROI in the short term can discourage managers from investing in new assets (since the average ROI of an investment centre tends to fall in the early stages of a new investment) even if the new investment is beneficial for the group as a whole (ie the investment's ROI is greater than the group's target rate of return). This focuses attention on short-run performance whereas investment decisions should be evaluated over their full life (which will normally be over the long term).	RI can help to overcome this problem of sub-optimality and lack of goal congruence by highlighting projects which return more than the cost of capital.
It can be difficult to compare percentage ROI results of investment centres if their activities are very different.	RI can overcome this problem through the use of different interest rates for different investment centres.

| Divisionalisation | Responsibility accounting | **Investment centre performance appraisal** |

Behavioural implications

During the time of their employment, managers like to ensure that their performance and the results of their decisions appear in the most favourable light. It is probable that they will have no regard for the later life of their investment centre's projects or for the overall performance of the group, with the following results.

- They will favour proposals that produce excellent results in the short term but are possibly unacceptable in the longer term.
- They will disregard proposals that are in the best interests of the group as a whole.

This type of performance measurement may therefore produce **dysfunctional decision making**. Managers will consider their own performance and not the longer-term interests of the investment centre or the interests of the group.

Example
A manager might decide to reduce investment and depreciation (and hence increase ROI) by scrapping some machinery not currently in use. When the machinery is eventually required, the manager would be obliged to buy new equipment.

Example
A manager might reject a project with an ROI of 30% if it causes the investment centre's ROI to fall from 38% to 35% even if the return is above the organisation's target of 25% (and hence the project is beneficial for the group as a whole).

Notes

Notes